Hello friend,

Thank you for purchasin_   .. ɔ. off, we would like to celebrate that 25% of the profits will be donated directly to the Scottish Mountain Rescue to continue their efforts. The rest will be given to the people who made this book possible: writers, researchers, editors, etc.

This is one of our first journals so it may not be perfect; we are simply a group of hikers who wanted a journal. If you would like to suggest any edits please get in touch at:

weemunroteam@gmail.com

We'll see you on the trail,

Wee Munro Team

IF FOUND PLEASE RETURN TO:

Name:

Telephone #:

Address:

_____

_____

_____

Contents

Rank	Munro	Elev.	Hiked	Winter
1.	Ben Nevis	1345m	☐	☐
2.	Ben Macdui	1309m	☐	☐
3.	Braeriach	1296m	☐	☐
4.	Cairn Toul	1291m	☐	☐
5.	Sgor an Lochan Uaine (The Angel's Peak)	1258m	☐	☐
6.	Cairn Gorm	1244m	☐	☐
7.	Aonach Beag	1234m	☐	☐
8.	Aonach Mor	1221m	☐	☐
9.	Carn Mor Dearg	1220m	☐	☐
10.	Ben Lawers	1214m	☐	☐
11.	Beinn a' Bhuird	1197m	☐	☐
12.	Carn Eighe	1183m	☐	☐
13.	Beinn Mheadhoin	1182m	☐	☐
14.	Mam Sodhail	1181m	☐	☐
15.	Stob Choire Claurigh	1177m	☐	☐
16.	Ben More (Glen Dochart)	1174m	☐	☐
17.	Ben Avon, Leabaoidh an Daimh Bhuide	1171m	☐	☐
18.	Stob Binnein	1165m	☐	☐
19.	Beinn Bhrotain	1157m	☐	☐
20.	Derry Cairngorm	1155m	☐	☐
21.	Lochnagar	1155m	☐	☐
22.	Sgurr nan Ceathreamhnan	1151m	☐	☐
23.	Bidean nam Bian	1150m	☐	☐

#	Munro	Elev.	Hiked	Winter
24.	Sgurr na Lapaich	1150m	☐	☐
25.	Ben Alder	1148m	☐	☐
26.	Geal-Charn	1132m	☐	☐
27.	Ben Lui (Beinn Laoigh)	1130m	☐	☐
28.	Binnein Mor	1130m	☐	☐
29.	An Riabhachan	1129m	☐	☐
30.	Creag Meagaidh	1128m	☐	☐
31.	Ben Cruachan	1126m	☐	☐
32.	Meall Garbh	1123m	☐	☐
33.	Carn nan Gabhar	1121m	☐	☐
34.	A' Chralaig	1120m	☐	☐
35.	Sgor Gaoith	1118m	☐	☐
36.	An Stuc	1117m	☐	☐
37.	Aonach Beag	1116m	☐	☐
38.	Stob Coire an Laoigh	1116m	☐	☐
39.	Stob Coire Easain	1115m	☐	☐
40.	Monadh Mor	1113m	☐	☐
41.	Tom a' Choinich	1112m	☐	☐
42.	Carn a' Choire Boidheach	1110m	☐	☐
43.	Sgurr Mor	1110m	☐	☐
44.	Sgurr nan Conbhairean	1109m	☐	☐
45.	Meall a' Bhuiridh	1108m	☐	☐
46.	Stob a' Choire Mheadhoin	1105m	☐	☐
47.	Beinn Ghlas	1103m	☐	☐
48.	Beinn Eibhinn	1102m	☐	☐
49.	Mullach Fraoch-choire	1102m	☐	☐
50.	Creise	1100m	☐	☐

#	Munro	Elev.	Hiked	Winter
51.	Sgurr a' Mhaim	1099m	☐	☐
52.	Sgurr Choinnich Mor	1094m	☐	☐
53.	Sgurr nan Clach Geala	1093m	☐	☐
54.	Bynack More	1090m	☐	☐
55.	Stob Ghabhar	1090m	☐	☐
56.	Beinn a' Chlachair	1087m	☐	☐
57.	Beinn Dearg	1084m	☐	☐
58.	Beinn a' Chaorainn	1083m	☐	☐
59.	Schiehallion	1083m	☐	☐
60.	Sgurr a' Choire Ghlais	1083m	☐	☐
61.	Beinn a' Chreachain	1081m	☐	☐
62.	Beinn Heasgarnich	1078m	☐	☐
63.	Ben Starav	1078m	☐	☐
64.	Beinn Dorain	1076m	☐	☐
65.	Stob Coire Sgreamach	1072m	☐	☐
66.	Braigh Coire Chruinn-bhalgain	1070m	☐	☐
67.	An Socach	1069m	☐	☐
68.	Meall Corranaich	1069m	☐	☐
69.	Glas Maol	1068m	☐	☐
70.	Sgurr Fhuaran	1067m	☐	☐
71.	Cairn of Claise	1064m	☐	☐
72.	Bidean a' Ghlas Thuill (An Teallach)	1062m	☐	☐
73.	Sgurr Fiona (An Teallach)	1060m	☐	☐
74.	Na Gruagaichean	1056m	☐	☐
75.	Spidean a Choire Leith (Liathach)	1055m	☐	☐
76.	Stob Poite Coire Ardair	1054m	☐	☐
77.	Toll Creagach	1054m	☐	☐

#	Munro	Elev.	Hiked	Winter
78.	Sgurr a' Chaorachain	1053m	☐	☐
79.	Beinn a' Chaorainn	1052m	☐	☐
80.	Glas Tulaichean	1051m	☐	☐
81.	Geal Charn	1049m	☐	☐
82.	Sgurr Fuar-thuill	1049m	☐	☐
83.	Carn an t-Sagairt Mor	1047m	☐	☐
84.	Creag Mhor	1047m	☐	☐
85.	Ben Wyvis, Glas Leathad Mor	1046m	☐	☐
86.	Chno Dearg	1046m	☐	☐
87.	Cruach Ardrain	1046m	☐	☐
88.	Beinn Iutharn Mhor	1045m	☐	☐
89.	Meall nan Tarmachan	1044m	☐	☐
90.	Stob Coire 'an Albannaich	1044m	☐	☐
91.	Carn Mairg	1041m	☐	☐
92.	Sgurr na Ciche	1040m	☐	☐
93.	Meall Ghaordie	1039m	☐	☐
94.	Beinn Achaladair	1038m	☐	☐
95.	Carn a' Mhaim	1037m	☐	☐
96.	Sgurr a' Bhealaich Dheirg	1036m	☐	☐
97.	Gleouraich	1035m	☐	☐
98.	Carn Dearg	1034m	☐	☐
99.	Am Bodach	1032m	☐	☐
100.	Beinn Fhada	1032m	☐	☐
101	Ben Oss	1029m	☐	☐
102	Carn an Righ	1029m	☐	☐
103	Carn Gorm	1029m	☐	☐
104.	Sgurr a' Mhaoraich	1027m	☐	☐

#	Munro	Elev.	Hiked	Winter
105.	Sgurr na Ciste Duibhe	1027m	☐	☐
106	Ben Challum	1025m	☐	☐
107.	Sgorr Dhearg (Beinn a' Bheithir)	1024m	☐	☐
108.	Mullach an Rathain (Liathach)	1023m	☐	☐
109	Aonach air Chrith	1021m	☐	☐
110.	Buachaille Etive Mor, Stob Dearg	1021m	☐	☐
111.	Ladhar Bheinn	1020m	☐	☐
112.	Beinn Bheoil	1019m	☐	☐
113.	Carn an Tuirc	1019m	☐	☐
114.	Mullach Clach a' Bhlair	1019m	☐	☐
115.	Mullach Coire Mhic Fhearchair	1018m	☐	☐
116.	Garbh Chioch Mhor	1013m	☐	☐
117.	Cairn Bannoch	1012m	☐	☐
118.	Beinn Udlamain	1011m	☐	☐
119.	Ben Ime	1011m	☐	☐
120.	Beinn Eighe (Ruadh-stac Mor)	1010m	☐	☐
121.	Sgurr an Doire Leathain	1010m	☐	☐
122.	Sgurr Eilde Mor	1010m	☐	☐
123.	The Saddle	1010m	☐	☐
124.	Beinn Dearg	1008m	☐	☐
125.	An Sgarsoch	1006m	☐	☐
126.	Carn Liath	1006m	☐	☐
127.	Beinn Fhionnlaidh	1005m	☐	☐
128.	Maoile Lunndaidh	1005m	☐	☐
129.	Beinn an Dothaidh	1004m	☐	☐
130.	Sgurr an Lochain	1004m	☐	☐

#	Munro	Elev.	Hiked	Winter
131.	The Devil's Point	1004m	☐	☐
132.	Sgurr Mor	1003m	☐	☐
133.	Sail Chaorainn	1002m	☐	☐
134.	Sgurr na Carnach	1002m	☐	☐
135.	Aonach Mheadhoin	1001m	☐	☐
136.	Meall Greigh	1001m	☐	☐
137.	Sgorr Dhonuill (Beinn a' Bheithir)	1001m	☐	☐
138.	Sgurr Breac	999m	☐	☐
139.	Sgurr Choinnich	999m	☐	☐
140.	Stob Ban	999m	☐	☐
141.	Ben More Assynt	998m	☐	☐
142.	Broad Cairn	998m	☐	☐
143.	Stob Diamh	998m	☐	☐
144.	A' Chailleach	997m	☐	☐
145.	Glas Bheinn Mhor	997m	☐	☐
146.	Spidean Mialach	996m	☐	☐
147.	An Caisteal	995m	☐	☐
148.	Carn an Fhidhleir	994m	☐	☐
149.	Sgor na h-Ulaidh	994m	☐	☐
150.	Sgurr na Ruaidhe	993m	☐	☐
151.	Spidean Coire nan Clach (Beinn Eighe)	993m	☐	☐
152.	Carn nan Gobhar (Glen Cannich)	992m	☐	☐
153.	Carn nan Gobhar (Glen Strathfarrar)	992m	☐	☐
154.	Sgurr Alasdair	992m	☐	☐
155.	Sgairneach Mhor	991m	☐	☐
156.	Beinn Eunaich	989m	☐	☐

#	Munro	Elev.	Hiked	Winter
157.	Sgurr Ban (Letterewe)	989m	☐	☐
158.	Conival	987m	☐	☐
159.	Creag Leachach	987m	☐	☐
160	Druim Shionnach	987m	☐	☐
161.	Gulvain	987m	☐	☐
162.	Lurg Mhor	986m	☐	☐
163.	Sgurr Dearg (The Inaccessible Pinnacle)	986m	☐	☐
164	Sgurr Mhor (Beinn Alligin)	986m	☐	☐
165.	Ben Vorlich (by Loch Earn)	985m	☐	☐
166	An Gearanach	982m	☐	☐
167.	Mullach na Dheiragain	982m	☐	☐
169	Maol Chinn-dearg	981m	☐	☐
169	Meall nan Aighean	981m	☐	☐
170.	Slioch – North Top	981m	☐	☐
171.	Stob Coire a' Chairn	981m	☐	☐
172.	Beinn a' Chochuill	980m	☐	☐
173.	Ciste Dhubh	979m	☐	☐
174.	Stob Coire Sgriodain	979m	☐	☐
175.	Beinn Dubhchraig	978m	☐	☐
176.	Cona' Mheall	978m	☐	☐
177.	Meall nan Ceapraichean	977m	☐	☐
178.	Stob Ban	977m	☐	☐
179.	A' Mharconaich	975m	☐	☐
180.	Carn a' Gheoidh	975m	☐	☐
181.	Carn Liath	975m	☐	☐
182.	Stuc a' Chroin	975m	☐	☐
183.	Beinn Sgritheall	974m	☐	☐

#	Munro	Elev.	Hiked	Winter
184.	Ben Lomond	974m	☐	☐
185.	Sgurr a' Ghreadhaidh	973m	☐	☐
186.	Meall Garbh	968m	☐	☐
187.	A' Mhaighdean	967m	☐	☐
188.	Sgorr nam Fiannaidh (Aonach Eagach)	967m	☐	☐
189.	Ben More	966m	☐	☐
190.	Sgurr na Banachdich	965m	☐	☐
191.	Sgurr nan Gillean	964m	☐	☐
192.	Carn a' Chlamain	963m	☐	☐
193.	Sgurr Thuilm	963m	☐	☐
194.	Ben Klibreck	962m	☐	☐
195.	Sgorr Ruadh	962m	☐	☐
196.	Beinn nan Aighenan	960m	☐	☐
197.	Stuchd an Lochain	960m	☐	☐
198.	Beinn Fhionnlaidh	959m	☐	☐
199.	Meall Glas	959m	☐	☐
200.	Bruach na Frithe	958m	☐	☐
201.	Buachaille Etive Beag, Stob Dubh	958m	☐	☐
202.	Tolmount	958m	☐	☐
203.	Carn Ghluasaid	957m	☐	☐
204.	Tom Buidhe	957m	☐	☐
205.	Buachaille Etive Mor, Stob na Broige	956m	☐	☐
206.	Saileag	956m	☐	☐
207.	Sgurr nan Coireachean	956m	☐	☐
208.	Sgor Gaibhre	955m	☐	☐
209.	Beinn Liath Mhor Fannaich	954m	☐	☐

#	Munro	Elev.	Hiked	Winter
210.	Am Faochagach	953m	☐	☐
211.	Beinn Mhanach	953m	☐	☐
212.	Meall Dearg (Aonach Eagach)	953m	☐	☐
213.	Sgurr nan Coireachan	953m	☐	☐
214.	Meall Chuaich	951m	☐	☐
215.	Meall Gorm	949m	☐	☐
216.	Beinn Bhuidhe	948m	☐	☐
217.	Sgurr Mhic Choinnich	948m	☐	☐
218.	Creag a' Mhaim	947m	☐	☐
219.	Driesh	947m	☐	☐
220.	Beinn Tulaichean	946m	☐	☐
221.	Carn Bhac	946m	☐	☐
222	Meall Buidhe	946m	☐	☐
223	Sgurr na Sgine	946m	☐	☐
224	Bidean a' Choire Sheasgaich	945m	☐	☐
225	Carn Dearg	945m	☐	☐
226	Stob a' Choire Odhair	945m	☐	☐
227	An Socach	944m	☐	☐
228	Sgurr Dubh Mor	944m	☐	☐
229	Ben Vorlich	943m	☐	☐
230	Binnean Beag	943m	☐	☐
231.	Beinn a' Chroin	942m	☐	☐
232	Carn Dearg	941m	☐	☐
233.	Carn na Caim	941m	☐	☐
234	Luinne Bheinne	939m	☐	☐
235	Mount Keen	939m	☐	☐
236	Mullach na Coirean	939m	☐	☐
237	Beinn Sgulaird	937m	☐	☐

#	Munro	Elev.	Hiked	Winter
238.	Beinn Tarsuinn	937m	☐	☐
239.	Sron a' Choire Ghairbh	937m	☐	☐
240.	A' Bhuidheanach Bheag	936m	☐	☐
241.	Beinn na Lap	935m	☐	☐
242.	Am Basteir	934m	☐	☐
243.	Meall a' Chrasgaidh	934m	☐	☐
244.	Beinn Chabhair	933m	☐	☐
245.	Fionn Bheinn	933m	☐	☐
246.	Maol Chean-dearg	933m	☐	☐
247.	The Cairnwell	933m	☐	☐
248.	Meall Buidhe	932m	☐	☐
249.	Beinn Bhreac	931m	☐	☐
250.	Ben Chonzie (Ben-y-Hone)	931m	☐	☐
251.	A' Chailleach	930m	☐	☐
252.	Bla Bheinn (Blaven)	928m	☐	☐
253.	Mayar	928m	☐	☐
254.	Meall nan Eun	928m	☐	☐
255.	Moruisg	928m	☐	☐
256.	Ben Hope	927m	☐	☐
257.	Eididh nan Clach Geala	927m	☐	☐
258.	Beinn Liath Mhor	926m	☐	☐
259.	Beinn Narnain	926m	☐	☐
260.	Geal Charn	926m	☐	☐
261.	Meall a Choire Leith	926m	☐	☐
262.	Seana Bhraigh	926m	☐	☐
263.	Buachaille Etive Beag, Stob Coire Raineach	925m	☐	☐
264.	Creag Pitridh	924m	☐	☐

#	Munro	Elev.	Hiked	Winter
265	Sgurr nan Eag	924m	☐	☐
266	An Coileachan	923m	☐	☐
267	Sgurr nan Each	923m	☐	☐
268.	Tom na Gruagaich (Beinn Alligin)	922m	☐	☐
269.	An Socach	921m	☐	☐
270.	Sgiath Chuil	921m	☐	☐
271.	Carn Sgulain	920m	☐	☐
272.	Gairich	919m	☐	☐
273.	Ruadh Stac Mor	919m	☐	☐
274.	A' Ghlas-bheinn	918m	☐	☐
275.	Creag nan Damh	918m	☐	☐
276.	Meall na Teanga	918m	☐	☐
277.	Sgurr a' Mhadaidh	918m	☐	☐
278.	Geal-charn	917m	☐	☐
279.	Beinn a' Chleibh	916m	☐	☐
280.	Ben Vane	916m	☐	☐
281.	Beinn Teallach	915m	☐	☐
282.	Carn Aosda	915m	☐	☐

*You may notice a repetition in names. This is because some Munros have multiple peaks. In other cases, this is because the Munros are geographically separate but share the same name. We have strived to not add any additional names or markers; this is to keep the integrity of the original name.

SCOTTISH MOUNTAIN RESCUE- ABOUT US

Scottish Mountain Rescue (SMR) represents 24 Mountain Rescue Teams (MRTs) made up of highly trained volunteers. Scottish Mountain Rescue and our member teams are all charities. In addition to representing these member MRTs, SMR also serves three Police Scotland MRTs and one RAF MRT.

Our 850 volunteers respond in a moment's notice, 24 hours a day, 365 days a year to provide assistance to people in the outdoors. They give up their time, their beds, abandon their work and are often called away from their families to assist total strangers.

SUPPORT

You can support Mountain Rescue in Scotland by fundraising or donating to your local team or to Scottish Mountain Rescue (3 in 5 rescues are funded by donations from the public). It is your support that helps us to be there for people in need of rescue in the mountains and ultimately saves lives.

To donate or for more information about us please visit our website at:
www.scottishmountainrescue.org/support-us

"Together we are here to save lives in the outdoors."

WHAT TO DO IF YOU HAVE AN ACCIDENT?

Only a very small number of walkers or climbers get into difficulty in the mountains, but you must be prepared and know what to do and who to call. If you are involved in an accident in the hills, the main thing is to:

1.Remain calm
2.Assess the situation
3. Decide what to do

- Make sure you and the group are not in immediate danger.
- Give first aid to the injured.
- Locate your exact position.
- Keep warm and decide whether to descend, find shelter, remain where you are, or call for help.

If you call for help in the mountains, call 999 or 112 and ask for the Police and Mountain Rescue.

The following information will be required;
- Location (6 figure grid reference or named location).
- Number of casualties and nature of injuries.
- Number in the group and what equipment the group have.
- Your phone number and the numbers of any other mobiles in the group.

Weak Signal Text Service

Register your mobile phone now with the 999 text service as, if the signal is weak, it still may be enough for a text message and these can only be accepted if the phone used has been pre-registered. It's simple to do: just text the word 'register' to 999. You will get a reply and should then follow the instructions you are sent. This will take about two minutes of your time and could save your life.

For more information please visit the Mountaineering Scotland website https://www.mountaineering.scot/safety-and-skills

Hardest Peaks

☆☆☆☆☆   ☆☆☆☆☆

- ⊕ A' Mhaighdean
- ⊕ Beinn Mhadaidh
- ⊕ Sgurr Dearg *(I.P.)*
- ⊕ Sgurr Alasdair
- ⊕ Bidein a'Choire Sheasgaich

- ⊕ Aonach Eagach
- ⊕ Sgurra'Mhadaidh
- ⊕ Sgurr nan Gillean
- ⊕ Liathach
- ⊕ Mullach na Dheiragain

- ⊕ Beinn Dorain
- ⊕ Ben Kilbreck
- ⊕ Ladhar Bheinn
- ⊕ Seana Bhraigh
- ⊕ Sgurr nan Ceathrearnhnan

Easiest Peaks

☆   ☆

- ⊕ Ben Chonzie
- ⊕ Ben Lomond
- ⊕ Cairnwell Trio
- ⊕ Schiehallion
- ⊕ Beinn a'Ghlo Range

- ⊕ Beinn Ghlas
- ⊕ Ben Vorlich
- ⊕ Glen Clova Duo
- ⊕ Buachaille Etive Beag

- ⊕ Ben Lawers
- ⊕ Ben Wyvis
- ⊕ Mount Keen
- ⊕ Meall nan Tarmachan (ridge)

These lists are in no particular order. DIfficulty is determined by many factors including but not limited to: Accessibility to and from the munro, weather conditions, terrain, elevation increase/decrease, path quality, infrastructure, etc...

Creag, crag:
A steep rugged mass of rock projecting upward or outward (a cliff).

Corrie:
A steep-sided channel at the head of a valley, or on a mountainside, formed by glacial erosion.

Carn, Cairn:
A mound of stones (built by people) to memorialise or identify a location. This could be: trail markers, burial sites, peaks, etc...

Sgurr:
Steep pointed hill coming to a sharp peak, or a large conical hill.

Sgor, Sgorr:
A sharp, isolated, steep peak, or a pinnacle.

Ben, Beinn, Bheinn, Ven, Vain:
Mountain, large mass

Stac, Bidean, Bidein, Bidhein, Spidean, Biod, Bioda, Binnean, Binnein:
Cone shaped peak (conical)

Dàn, Bhàn, Bhàin, Fionn, Geal:
White (or light coloured)

Buachaille:
Shepherd

Dubh Dhubh, Duibh, Dhuibh, Duibhe, Dubha:
Black

Druim, Aonach, Leathad, Leitir, Gualann, Imir, Socach, Sròn:
A long narrow hilltop, a ridge or crest. Furthermore at a great height it may be referred to as a Leathad or if wide Leitir may be used. Generally Socach is the end of a ridge meaning, snout, beak or nose.

Meall, Mheall, Mill, Mhill, Maol, Maoile, Ceann, Chean, Cinn, Chinn:
All very common descriptions of a bare round rocky hill. Maol, Maoile usually is translated as bald head or bald top.

Cruach, Cruaiche, Tòrr, Cleit:
Usually translated as stack, heap, mound or pile.

Cnoc, Chnoc, Chnuic, Bàrr, Cnap, Ord, Uird, Tulach, Tulaich, Tulaichean, Tom, Guirean, Màm, Mhàim, Cìoch, Cìche:
Any rounded hill (regardless of size) that resemblances a pimple or breast.

Meadhoin, Meadhain, Mheadhoin, Mheadhain, Meadhonach, Meadhanach, Mheadhonach, Mheadhanach, Vane:
Middle

Breac, Bhreac, Riabhach, Riabhaich:
Speckled or spotted upper part of the hill.

Dearg, Dhearg, Deirg, Dheirg, Ruadh Ruaidh:
Red

Odhar, Odhair, Donn:
Brownish

Buidhe, Bhuidhe, Or, Oir:
Yellow ("Or" and "Oir" mean gold)

Glas, Ghlas, Ghlais, Lìath:
Greyish-Greenish-Blue

Mòr, Mhòr, Mhòir, More:
Great, big, large or grand.

Beag, Bheag, Bhig, Beg:
Small or little

Gabhar, Gobhar, Ghabhar, Gaibhre:
Goat

Damh, Daimh, Diamh, Boc, Buic, Bhuic:
Damh, Daimh, Diamh all mean stag, where as Boc, Buic, Bhuic mean buck. The term can be for "roaring" + "rutting", or simply stating there are bucks/stags on that Munro.

Fiadh, Fèidh, Earb, Earba:
Fiadh, Feidh mean deer in general (male or female) and Earb + Earba mean a female deer.

Bealach, Bhealaich, Màm, Mhàim:
The Lowest point between two peaks (a mountain pass or col).

Cruach, Cruaiche, Tòrr, Cleit:
Stack, heap, mound or pile.

Gaelic often has the same word with slightly different spellings. This has been attributed to mis-translations and/or geographically different spellings of the same word. There is also different pronunciations in regards to accents from one village/town to another which affected the translation.

Your Access Rights: Scottish Outdoor Access Code, 2005

Everyone, whatever their age or ability, has access rights established by the Land Reform (Scotland) Act of 2003. You only have access rights if you exercise them responsibility.

You can exercise these rights, provided you do so responsibly, over most land and inland water in Scotland, including mountains, moorland, woods and forests, grassland, margins of fields in which crops are growing, paths and tracks, rivers and lochs, the coast and most parks and open spaces. Access rights can be exercised at any time of the day or night.

You can exercise access rights for recreational purposes (such as pastimes, family and social activities, and more active pursuits like horse riding, cycling, wild camping and taking part in events), educational purposes (concerned with furthering a person's understanding of the natural and cultural heritage), some commercial purposes (where the activities are the same as those done by the general public) and for crossing over land or water.

You can also exercise access rights above or below the land (for example, you can exercise access rights in the air and in caves). Access rights equally extend underwater and on the surface.

 Know your rights and stay within them.

The Main Places Where Access Rights Do Not Apply Are:

Houses and gardens, and non-residential buildings and associated land; land in which crops are growing; land next to a school and used by the school; sports or playing fields when these are in use and where the exercise of access rights would interfere with such use; land developed and in use for recreation and where the exercise of access rights would interfere with such use; golf courses (but you can cross a golf course provided you don't interfere with any games of golf); places like airfields, railways, telecommunications sites, military bases and installations, working quarries and construction sites; and visitor attractions or other places which charge for entry.

Access Rights Do Not Extend To:

Being on or crossing land for the purpose of doing anything which is an offence, such as theft, breach of the peace, nuisance, poaching, allowing a dog to worry livestock, dropping litter, polluting water or disturbing certain wild birds, animals and plants; hunting,shooting or fishing; any form of motorised recreation or passage (except by people with a disability using a vehicle or vessel adapted for their use); anyone responsible for a dog which is not under proper control; or to anyone taking away anything from the land for a commercial purpose.

3 Key Principles:

1. **Respect the Interests of Other People.** Acting with courtesy, consideration and awareness is very important. If you are exercising access rights, make sure that you respect the privacy, safety and livelihoods of those living or working in the outdoors, and the needs of other people enjoying the outdoors.

2. **Care for the Environment.** If you are exercising access rights, look after the places you visit and enjoy, and leave the land as you find it.

3. **Take Responsibility for your own actions.** If you are exercising access rights, remember that the outdoors cannot be made risk-free and act with care at all times for your own safety and that of others.

More Information:

For more information and to read the full code, please visit:

https://www.outdooraccess-scotland.scot/

It would be irresponsible and unethical to tell people exactly where to wild camp. These locations would become overrun, and without the proper infrastructure would eventually become uninhabitable due to human excrement and rubbish; which would have long lasting effects on the vegetation. It would affect your experience of wild camping and would also cause local landowners trouble and frustration to no end. As such, we want to help you further your education on where **NOT** to wild camp.

The Outdoor Access Code Says:

Access rights extend to wild camping. This type of camping is lightweight, done in small numbers and only for two or three nights in any one place. You can camp in this way wherever access rights apply, but help to avoid causing problems for local people and land managers by not camping in enclosed fields of crops or farm animals and by keeping well away from buildings, roads or historic structures. Take extra care to avoid disturbing deer stalking or grouse shooting. If you wish to camp close to a house or building, seek the owner's permission.

Choosing a sight:

Most hikers think that sleeping one night anywhere has such little impact that it can't be bad and in some instances this might be true. But, if you think about how many people hike certain munros every year, then every 10 years, and if everyone chose the same spots, then there would be no grass, shrubs or wildlife left in those areas. When choosing a tent site for the night please help us by following these guidelines:

Camp Site Guidelines:

- In busy, high traffic areas, please use official campsites (it's a few quid but makes a huge difference).

- Find discreet places to camp (while following the law) and not hotspots posted online that tend to be overused.
- Practice "LEAVE NO TRACE", meaning not leaving: food scraps (even if buried), bits of rope, tent pegs, tree carvings, smoldering fires, stone circle fire places, cardboard, cans, plastic, wrappers, etc..
- Please keep noise to a minimum. Other people may be close by and noise travels easily in the hills (especially late night gatherings as noise travels particularly far at night).
- At no point, no matter where you are, is it ever appropriate to cut down wood, shrubs, saplings or any living thing. If you are concerned about other campers destroying vegetation you can contact the local police department.

Fires:

Never light an open fire during prolonged dry periods, in areas such as forests, woods, farmland, on peaty ground, near to buildings or in cultural heritage sites where damage can be easily caused. Heed all advice at times of high risk. Remove all traces of an open fire before you leave and extinguish fires to the point of no heat or smoke coming off the embers/ashes.

Fires In Camping Management Zones:

"No person shall without lawful authority; **light or cause a fire within a Management Zone** causing damage or likely to cause damage to a Management Zone; **or collect or use wood** from within a Management Zone that causes damage or is likely to cause damage to a Management Zone."

For more information on management zones throughout the UK, please visit: www.mountaineering.scot

Going to the Toilet:

There will be millions of people that hike the same trail you are taking and if everyone went to the toilet near the trail there would be knee high walls of human waste all the way from access, to summit. So please, when possible use public toilets. In the unlikely event you cannot hold it, we ask you to use the following guidelines:

- *When going to the toilet walk at least 30m/100ft away from any water source (rivers, bogs, ponds, lochs, etc…) or any trails.*
- *In lowland areas please bury your excrement in a small hole (not under boulders or hidden from sight with leaves). In highland areas (e.g. on a Munro or at high altitudes) please cover any excrement with a small pile of stones as vegetation in these areas can take a long time to recover. (Extreme caution is needed in these areas...if possible hold it until you get down).*
- *Tampons and sanitary towels should not be buried, as this is littering and can face a **fine of up to £2,500** (not to mention within a few hours an animal will dig it up, exposing it to the next walkers). Instead, place them in a container (or tin foil is also great) with a tea bag, or bicarbonate soda, this will absorb odours and liquid. Usually, within a few hours, you will come to a place where you can dispose of it in a rubbish bin.*

Loch Lomond and the Trossachs National Park:

During the months of March to September, seasonal camping management byelaws are in place within Loch Lomond & the Trossachs National Park which will determine where you are able to wild camp. In respect to Loch Lomond, these byelaws are in place from Drymen to beyond Rowardennan, and also at the northern end of the loch around the Inverarnan area. Camping within these zones requires booking at a campsite or at a wild camping permit area. Failure to comply with the byelaws may result in you be charged and fined up to £500. For more information on the byelaws and the areas affected please visit www.lochlomond-trossachs.org

In Summary:

The Scottish Outdoors is beautiful, but can be dangerous, and is more fragile than people realise. We all need to do our part in keeping it the way it is (or better). If you are in doubt about your actions or don't know the best way to do something, please take it upon yourself to research the correct methods. There are great resources available making access to the information easy.

Resources:

- www.outdooraccess-scotland.scot
- www.mountaineering.scot
- http://www.walkscotland.com/
- www.trespass.com/advice/wild-camping-legal/
- www.lochlomond-trossachs.org

By providing these resources we do not condone the ideas, mindsets, opinions or actions of these websites/their partners or members. At the time of publishing they had some great information and provided a worthwhile read into sustainable camping practices. However, websites can change in a blink of an eye, and that is why we are adding a caution.

More Information:

For legal guidelines and to read the full code, please visit:

https://www.outdooraccess-scotland.scot/

HOW TO NAVIGATE THIS BOOK

There are 3 ways in which you can navigate this book: **by height**, **alphabetically** and **regionally.**

Height: The entry pages themselves are organized by height. Simply flip through the pages until you get to your desired height then pay attention to the names.

Alphabetical: If you wish to navigate alphabetically you must first know the spelling of the Munro (the more precise the better as a lot share similar names). Then proceed to the alphabetical index **(page 312)**. Please keep in mind some Munros have the same names so double check against region and height.

Regional: If you have an idea of the region you would like to hike in, then go to the regional index **(page 317)**. You will see all the Munros in that region allowing you to plan for bagging more than 1 in a day. You will find a map **on page 322** to further assist you with this.

Ben Nevis
Venomous
(1345m)

Summer Ascent: ☐☐☐☐☐
Winter Ascent: ☐☐☐☐☐

Trailhead: _____

Hill #: 01

Region #: 04

Date:

Time:

Weather:

Companions:

Future Advice:

_____
_____
_____
_____
_____
_____
_____
_____
_____
_____
_____
_____
_____

Ben Macdui
Hill of the son of Duff
(1309m)

Hill #: 02

Region #: 08

Summer Ascent: ☐☐☐☐☐
Winter Ascent: ☐☐☐☐☐
Trailhead: _____

Date:

Time:

Weather:

Companions:

Future Advice:

_____

_____

_____

_____

_____

_____

_____

_____

_____

_____

_____

Braeriach
Brindled greyish upper part
(1296m)

Summer Ascent: ☐☐☐☐☐

Winter Ascent: ☐☐☐☐☐

Hill #: 03

Region #: 08

Trailhead: _____

Date:

Time:

Weather:

Companions:

Future Advice:

Cairn Toul
Hill of the barn
(1291m)

Hill #: 04

Region #: 08

Summer Ascent: ☐☐☐☐☐
Winter Ascent: ☐☐☐☐☐
Trailhead: _____

Date:

Time:

Weather:

Companions:

Future Advice:

_____
_____
_____
_____
_____
_____
_____
_____
_____
_____
_____

Sgor an Lochan Uaine
(The Angel's Peak)
Peak of the little green loch
(1258m)

Summer Ascent: ☐☐☐☐☐

Winter Ascent: ☐☐☐☐☐

Hill #: 05

Trailhead: _____

Region #: 08

Date:

Time:

Weather:

Companions:

Future Advice:

_____
_____
_____
_____
_____
_____
_____
_____
_____
_____
_____
_____

Cairn Gorm
Blue-green hill
(1244m)

Summer Ascent: ☐☐☐☐☐
Winter Ascent: ☐☐☐☐☐

Trailhead: _____

Date:

Time:

Weather:

Companions:

Future Advice:

Aonach Beag
Little hill (or small ridge)
(1234m)

Summer Ascent: ☐☐☐☐☐
Winter Ascent: ☐☐☐☐☐

Trailhead: _____

Hill #: 07

Region #: 04

Date:

Time:

Weather:

Companions:

Future Advice:

_____

_____

_____

_____

_____

_____

_____

_____

_____

_____

_____

Aonach Mor
Big hill (or big ridge)
(1221m)

Hill #: 08

Region #: 04

Summer Ascent: ☐☐☐☐☐
Winter Ascent: ☐☐☐☐☐
Trailhead: _____

Date:

Time:

Weather:

Companions:

Future Advice:

_____
_____
_____
_____
_____
_____
_____
_____
_____
_____
_____
_____

Carn Mor Dearg
Big red hill
(1220m)

Summer Ascent: ☐☐☐☐☐
Winter Ascent: ☐☐☐☐☐

Trailhead: _____

Date:

Time:

Weather:

Companions:

Future Advice:

_____

_____

_____

_____

_____

_____

_____

_____

_____

_____

_____

_____

Ben Lawers
Hill of the loud stream (or hoof hill)
(1214m)

Hill #: **10**

Summer Ascent: ☐☐☐☐☐
Winter Ascent: ☐☐☐☐☐

Region #: **02**

Trailhead: _____

Date:

Time:

Weather:

Companions:

Future Advice:

_____
_____
_____
_____
_____
_____
_____
_____
_____
_____
_____
_____

Beinn a' Bhuird
Table-hill
(1197m)

Summer Ascent: ☐☐☐☐☐
Winter Ascent: ☐☐☐☐☐

Trailhead: _____

Hill #: **11**

Region #: **08**

Date:

Time:

Weather:

Companions:

Future Advice:

_____

_____

_____

_____

_____

_____

_____

_____

_____

_____

_____

_____

Carn Eighe
File hill (or notch hill)
(1183m)

Hill #: **12**

Region #: **11**

Summer Ascent: ☐☐☐☐☐
Winter Ascent: ☐☐☐☐☐
Trailhead: _____

Date:

Time:

Weather:

Companions:

Future Advice:

_____

_____

_____

_____

_____

_____

_____

_____

_____

_____

_____

Beinn Mheadhoin
Middle hill
(1182m)

Summer Ascent: ☐☐☐☐☐

Winter Ascent: ☐☐☐☐☐

Trailhead: _____

Hill #: **13**

Region #: **08**

Date:

Time:

Weather:

Companions:

Future Advice:

_____
_____
_____
_____
_____
_____
_____
_____
_____
_____
_____
_____
_____
_____

Mam Sodhail
Hill of the barns
(1181m)

Hill #: **14**

Region #: **11**

Summer Ascent: ☐☐☐☐☐
Winter Ascent: ☐☐☐☐☐
Trailhead: _____

Date:

Time:

Weather:

Companions:

Future Advice:

_____
_____
_____
_____
_____
_____
_____
_____
_____
_____
_____

Stob Choire Claurigh
Peak of the brawling or clamouring (corrie)
(1177m)

Summer Ascent: ☐☐☐☐☐
Winter Ascent: ☐☐☐☐☐

Hill #: 15

Region #: 04

Trailhead: _____

Date:

Time:

Weather:

Companions:

Future Advice:

_____
_____
_____
_____
_____
_____
_____
_____
_____
_____
_____
_____
_____

Ben More (Glen Dochart)
Big hill
(1174m)

Hill #: 16

Region #: 01

Summer Ascent: ☐☐☐☐☐
Winter Ascent: ☐☐☐☐☐

Trailhead: _____

Date:

Time:

Weather:

Companions:

Future Advice:

_____

_____

_____

_____

_____

_____

_____

_____

_____

_____

_____

_____

Ben Avon
(Leabaoidh an Daimh Bhuide)
Bed of the yellow stag (or of the bright one)
(1171m)

Summer Ascent: ☐☐☐☐☐

Winter Ascent: ☐☐☐☐☐

Hill #: 17

Trailhead: _____

Region #: 08

Date:

Time:

Weather:

Companions:

Future Advice:

_____

_____

_____

_____

_____

_____

_____

_____

_____

_____

_____

_____

_____

Stob Binnein
Cone Shaped peak (or peak of the anvil)
(1165m)

Hill #: **18**

Region #: **01**

Summer Ascent: ☐☐☐☐☐
Winter Ascent: ☐☐☐☐☐
Trailhead: _____

Date:

Time:

Weather:

Companions:

Future Advice:

_____
_____
_____
_____
_____
_____
_____
_____
_____
_____
_____
_____

Beinn Bhrotain
Hill of the mastiff (war dog)
(1157m)

Summer Ascent: ☐☐☐☐☐
Winter Ascent: ☐☐☐☐☐

Trailhead: _____

Hill #: 19

Region #: 08

Date:

Time:

Weather:

Companions:

Future Advice:

_____
_____
_____
_____
_____
_____
_____
_____
_____
_____
_____
_____

Derry Cairngorm
Blue hill (or cairn) of Derry
(1155m)

Hill #: 20

Region #: 08

Summer Ascent: ☐☐☐☐☐
Winter Ascent: ☐☐☐☐☐

Trailhead: _____

Date:

Time:

Weather:

Companions:

Future Advice:

_____

_____

_____

_____

_____

_____

_____

_____

_____

_____

_____

_____

Lochnagar
Little loch of the noisy sound (pre-1700s Mountain of the breast)
(1155m)

Summer Ascent: ☐☐☐☐☐

Winter Ascent: ☐☐☐☐☐

Trailhead: _____

Hill #: 21

Region #: 07

Date:

Time:

Weather:

Companions:

Future Advice:

_____
_____
_____
_____
_____
_____
_____
_____
_____
_____
_____
_____
_____
_____

Sgurr nan Ceathreamhnan
Peak of the quarters (divided land)
(1151m)

Summer Ascent: ☐☐☐☐☐
Winter Ascent: ☐☐☐☐☐
Trailhead: _____

Date:

Time:

Weather:

Companions:

Future Advice:

_____

_____

_____

_____

_____

_____

_____

_____

_____

_____

_____

Bidean nam Bian

Peak of the mountains (or peak of the animal pelts)
(1150m)

Summer Ascent: ☐☐☐☐☐

Winter Ascent: ☐☐☐☐☐

Trailhead: _____

Date:

Time:

Weather:

Companions:

Future Advice:

_____
_____
_____
_____
_____
_____
_____
_____
_____
_____
_____
_____
_____

Sgurr na Lapaich
Peak of the bog
(1150m)

Hill #: **24**

Region #: **12**

Summer Ascent: ☐☐☐☐☐
Winter Ascent: ☐☐☐☐☐
Trailhead: _____

Date:

Time:

Weather:

Companions:

Future Advice:

_____

_____

_____

_____

_____

_____

_____

_____

_____

_____

_____

_____

_____

Ben Alder
Hill of rock (&) water
(1148m)

Summer Ascent: ☐☐☐☐☐
Winter Ascent: ☐☐☐☐☐

Hill #: 25

Trailhead: _____

Region #: 04

Date:

Time:

Weather:

Companions:

Future Advice:

_____
_____
_____
_____
_____
_____
_____
_____
_____
_____
_____
_____
_____
_____

Geal–Charn
White hill
(1132m)

Hill #: 26

Region #: 04

Summer Ascent: ☐☐☐☐☐
Winter Ascent: ☐☐☐☐☐
Trailhead: _____

Date:

Time:

Weather:

Companions:

Future Advice:

Ben Lui (Beinn Laoigh)
Calf hill
(1130m)

Summer Ascent: ☐☐☐☐☐

Winter Ascent: ☐☐☐☐☐

Trailhead: _____

Hill #: 27

Region #: 01

Date:

Time:

Weather:

Companions:

Future Advice:

_____
_____
_____
_____
_____
_____
_____
_____
_____
_____
_____
_____
_____

Binnein Mor
Big peak
(1130m)

Summer Ascent: ☐☐☐☐☐
Winter Ascent: ☐☐☐☐☐
Trailhead: _____

Date:

Time:

Weather:

Companions:

Future Advice:

_____
_____
_____
_____
_____
_____
_____
_____
_____
_____
_____
_____

An Riabhachan
The brindled greyish one
(1129m)

Summer Ascent: ☐☐☐☐☐
Winter Ascent: ☐☐☐☐☐

Hill #: 29

Trailhead: _____

Region #: 12

Date:

Time:

Weather:

Companions:

Future Advice:

_____

_____

_____

_____

_____

_____

_____

_____

_____

_____

_____

_____

_____

Creag Meagaidh
Bogland rock (or bogland creag)
(1128m)

Hill #: 30

Region #: 09

Summer Ascent: ☐☐☐☐☐
Winter Ascent: ☐☐☐☐☐

Trailhead: _____

Date:

Time:

Weather:

Companions:

Future Advice:

_____
_____
_____
_____
_____
_____
_____
_____
_____
_____
_____
_____
_____

Ben Cruachan
Stacky hill (or mountain of the cone shaped peaks)
(1126m)

Summer Ascent: ☐☐☐☐☐

Winter Ascent: ☐☐☐☐☐

Trailhead: _____

Date:

Time:

Weather:

Companions:

Future Advice:

Meall Garbh
Rough hill
(1123m)

Summer Ascent: ☐☐☐☐☐
Winter Ascent: ☐☐☐☐☐

Trailhead: _____

Date:

Time:

Weather:

Companions:

Future Advice:

_____

_____

_____

_____

_____

_____

_____

_____

_____

_____

_____

_____

Carn nan Gabhar
Hill of the goats
(1121m)

Summer Ascent: ☐☐☐☐☐
Winter Ascent: ☐☐☐☐☐

Trailhead: _____

Hill #: **33**

Region #: **06**

Date:

Time:

Weather:

Companions:

Future Advice:

_____

_____

_____

_____

_____

_____

_____

_____

_____

_____

_____

_____

_____

_____

A' Chralaig
The basket (or creel)
(1120m)

Hill #: **34**

Region #: **11**

Summer Ascent: ☐☐☐☐☐
Winter Ascent: ☐☐☐☐☐

Trailhead: _____

Date:

Time:

Weather:

Companions:

Future Advice:

_____
_____
_____
_____
_____
_____
_____
_____
_____
_____
_____
_____
_____

Sgor Gaoith
Peak of wind (or windy peak)
(1118m)

Summer Ascent: ☐☐☐☐☐
Winter Ascent: ☐☐☐☐☐

Trailhead: _____

Hill #: **35**

Region #: **08**

Date:

Time:

Weather:

Companions:

Future Advice:

_____

_____

_____

_____

_____

_____

_____

_____

_____

_____

_____

_____

An Stuc
the peak
(1117m)

Summer Ascent: ☐☐☐☐☐
Winter Ascent: ☐☐☐☐☐
Trailhead: _____

Date:

Time:

Weather:

Companions:

Future Advice:

_____
_____
_____
_____
_____
_____
_____
_____
_____
_____
_____

Aonach Beag
Little hill (or little ridge)
(1116m)

Summer Ascent: ☐☐☐☐☐
Winter Ascent: ☐☐☐☐☐

Trailhead: _____

Hill #: 37

Region #: 04

Date:

Time:

Weather:

Companions:

Future Advice:

_____
_____
_____
_____
_____
_____
_____
_____
_____
_____
_____
_____
_____
_____
_____

Stob Coire an Laoigh
Peak of the corrie of the calf
(1116m)

Hill #: **38**

Region #: **04**

Summer Ascent: ☐☐☐☐☐
Winter Ascent: ☐☐☐☐☐

Trailhead: _____

Date:

Time:

Weather:

Companions:

Future Advice:

_____

_____

_____

_____

_____

_____

_____

_____

_____

_____

_____

_____

Stob Coire Easain
Peak of the corrie of the waterfall
(1115m)

Summer Ascent: ☐☐☐☐☐

Winter Ascent: ☐☐☐☐☐

Trailhead: _____

Date:

Time:

Weather:

Companions:

Future Advice:

_____

Monadh Mor
Big hill
(1113m)

Hill #: **40**

Region #: **08**

Summer Ascent: ☐☐☐☐☐
Winter Ascent: ☐☐☐☐☐

Trailhead: _____

Date:

Time:

Weather:

Companions:

Future Advice:

_____
_____
_____
_____
_____
_____
_____
_____
_____
_____
_____
_____

Tom a' Choinich
Hill of the moss
(1112m)

Summer Ascent: ☐☐☐☐☐
Winter Ascent: ☐☐☐☐☐

Hill #: **41**

Region #: **11**

Trailhead: _____

Date:

Time:

Weather:

Companions:

Future Advice:

_____

_____

_____

_____

_____

_____

_____

_____

_____

_____

_____

_____

_____

Carn a' Choire Boidheach
Hill of the beautiful corrie
(1110m)

Hill #: 42

Region #: 07

Summer Ascent: ☐☐☐☐☐
Winter Ascent: ☐☐☐☐☐
Trailhead: _____

Date:

Time:

Weather:

Companions:

Future Advice:

_____
_____
_____
_____
_____
_____
_____
_____
_____
_____
_____
_____

Sgurr Mor
Big peak
(1110m)

Summer Ascent: ☐☐☐☐☐

Winter Ascent: ☐☐☐☐☐

Trailhead: _____

Date:

Time:

Weather:

Companions:

Future Advice:

_____

_____

_____

_____

_____

_____

_____

_____

_____

_____

_____

_____

_____

_____

_____

Sgurr nan Conbhairean
Keeper of the hounds peak
(1109m)

Hill #: 44

Region #: 11

Summer Ascent: ☐☐☐☐☐
Winter Ascent: ☐☐☐☐☐
Trailhead: _____

Date:

Time:

Weather:

Companions:

Future Advice:

Meall a' Bhuiridh
Hill of the bellowing (of stags)
(1108m)

Summer Ascent: ☐☐☐☐☐

Winter Ascent: ☐☐☐☐☐

Trailhead: _____

Date:

Time:

Weather:

Companions:

Future Advice:

_____
_____
_____
_____
_____
_____
_____
_____
_____
_____
_____
_____
_____
_____
_____

Stob a' Choire Mheadhoin
Peak of the middle corrie
(1105m)

Hill #: **46**

Region #: **04**

Summer Ascent: ☐☐☐☐☐
Winter Ascent: ☐☐☐☐☐
Trailhead: _____

Date:

Time:

Weather:

Companions:

Future Advice:

_____
_____
_____
_____
_____
_____
_____
_____
_____
_____
_____
_____

Beinn Ghlas
Greenish-grey hill
(1103m)

Summer Ascent: ☐☐☐☐☐

Winter Ascent: ☐☐☐☐☐

Trailhead: _____

Hill #: **47**

Region #: **02**

Date:

Time:

Weather:

Companions:

Future Advice:

Beinn Eibhinn
Delightful hill
(1102m)

Summer Ascent: ☐☐☐☐☐
Winter Ascent: ☐☐☐☐☐

Trailhead: _____

Date:

Time:

Weather:

Companions:

Future Advice:

Mullach Fraoch
Heather-corrie peak
(1102m)

Summer Ascent: ☐☐☐☐☐
Winter Ascent: ☐☐☐☐☐

Trailhead: _____

Hill #: 49

Region #: 11

Date:

Time:

Weather:

Companions:

Future Advice:

_____
_____
_____
_____
_____
_____
_____
_____
_____
_____
_____
_____
_____

Creise
Unknown (maybe narrow?)
(1100m)

Hill #: 50

Region #: 03

Summer Ascent: ☐☐☐☐☐
Winter Ascent: ☐☐☐☐☐
Trailhead: _____

Date:

Time:

Weather:

Companions:

Future Advice:

_____
_____
_____
_____
_____
_____
_____
_____
_____
_____
_____
_____

Sgurr a' Mhaim
Peak of the large rounded hill
(1099m)

Summer Ascent: ☐☐☐☐☐
Winter Ascent: ☐☐☐☐☐

Trailhead: _____

Date:

Time:

Weather:

Companions:

Future Advice:

_____
_____
_____
_____
_____
_____
_____
_____
_____
_____
_____
_____
_____
_____

Sgurr Choinnich Mor
Big peak of the moss
(1094m)

Hill #: 52

Region #: 04

Summer Ascent: ☐☐☐☐☐
Winter Ascent: ☐☐☐☐☐
Trailhead: _____

Date:

Time:

Weather:

Companions:

Future Advice:

_____
_____
_____
_____
_____
_____
_____
_____
_____
_____
_____

Sgurr nan Clach Geala
Peak of the white stones
(1093m)

Summer Ascent: ☐☐☐☐☐
Winter Ascent: ☐☐☐☐☐

Hill #: 53

Region #: 14

Trailhead: _____

Date:

Time:

Weather:

Companions:

Future Advice:

_____
_____
_____
_____
_____
_____
_____
_____
_____
_____
_____
_____
_____

Bynack More
Obscure (or big cup)
(1090m)

Hill #: **54**

Region #: **08**

Summer Ascent: ☐☐☐☐☐
Winter Ascent: ☐☐☐☐☐

Trailhead: _____

Date:

Time:

Weather:

Companions:

Future Advice:

_____
_____
_____
_____
_____
_____
_____
_____
_____
_____
_____
_____
_____

Stob Ghabhar
Goat peak
(1090m)

Summer Ascent: ☐☐☐☐☐
Winter Ascent: ☐☐☐☐☐

Trailhead: _____

Hill #: 55

Region #: 03

Date:

Time:

Weather:

Companions:

Future Advice:

_____

_____

_____

_____

_____

_____

_____

_____

_____

_____

_____

_____

Beinn a' Chlachair
Stonemason's hill
(1087m)

Hill #: 56

Region #: 04

Summer Ascent: ☐☐☐☐☐
Winter Ascent: ☐☐☐☐☐

Trailhead: _____

Date:

Time:

Weather:

Companions:

Future Advice:

_____
_____
_____
_____
_____
_____
_____
_____
_____
_____
_____
_____

Beinn Dearg
Red hill
(1084m)

Summer Ascent: ☐☐☐☐☐
Winter Ascent: ☐☐☐☐☐

Trailhead: _____

Hill #: 57

Region #: 15

Date:

Time:

Weather:

Companions:

Future Advice:

_____
_____
_____
_____
_____
_____
_____
_____
_____
_____
_____
_____
_____

Beinn a' Chaorainn
Hill of the rowan (tree)
(1083m)

Hill #: 58

Region #: 08

Summer Ascent: ☐☐☐☐☐
Winter Ascent: ☐☐☐☐☐
Trailhead: _____

Date:

Time:

Weather:

Companions:

Future Advice:

Schiehallion
The fairly hill of the Caledonians
(1083m)

Summer Ascent: ☐☐☐☐☐

Winter Ascent: ☐☐☐☐☐

Trailhead: _____

Hill #: 59

Region #: 02

Date:

Time:

Weather:

Companions:

Future Advice:

_____

_____

_____

_____

_____

_____

_____

_____

_____

_____

_____

_____

_____

Sgurr a' Choire Ghlais
Peak of the greenish-grey corrie
(1083m)

Hill #: 60

Region #: 12

Summer Ascent: ☐☐☐☐☐
Winter Ascent: ☐☐☐☐☐
Trailhead: _____

Date:

Time:

Weather:

Companions:

Future Advice:

_____
_____
_____
_____
_____
_____
_____
_____
_____
_____
_____
_____

Beinn a' Chreachain
Hill of the rock (or hill of the clamshell)
(1081m)

Summer Ascent: ☐☐☐☐☐

Winter Ascent: ☐☐☐☐☐

Trailhead: _____

Hill #: 61

Region #: 02

Date:

Time:

Weather:

Companions:

Future Advice:

_____

_____

_____

_____

_____

_____

_____

_____

_____

_____

_____

_____

_____

_____

Beinn Heasgarnich
Sheltering hill (or peaceful hill)
(1078m)

Summer Ascent: ☐☐☐☐☐
Winter Ascent: ☐☐☐☐☐

Trailhead: _____

Date:

Time:

Weather:

Companions:

Future Advice:

_____

_____

_____

_____

_____

_____

_____

_____

_____

_____

_____

Ben Starav
Hill of the rustling noise?
(1078m)

Summer Ascent: ☐☐☐☐☐
Winter Ascent: ☐☐☐☐☐

Trailhead: _____

Date:

Time:

Weather:

Companions:

Future Advice:

_____
_____
_____
_____
_____
_____
_____
_____
_____
_____
_____
_____
_____
_____
_____
_____

Beinn Dorain
Hill of the streamlet (or otter)
(1076m)

Summer Ascent: ☐☐☐☐☐
Winter Ascent: ☐☐☐☐☐
Trailhead: _____

Date:

Time:

Weather:

Companions:

Future Advice:

_____

_____

_____

_____

_____

_____

_____

_____

_____

_____

_____

_____

Stob Coire Sgreamach
Peak of the dreadful (aweful) corrie
(1072m)

Summer Ascent: ☐☐☐☐☐

Winter Ascent: ☐☐☐☐☐

Hill #: 65

Trailhead: _____

Region #: 03

Date:

Time:

Weather:

Companions:

Future Advice:

_____

_____

_____

_____

_____

_____

_____

_____

_____

_____

_____

_____

_____

_____

Braigh Coire Chruinn–bhalgain
Upland of the corrie of the round blisters
(1070m)

Hill #: **66**

Region #: **06**

Summer Ascent: ☐☐☐☐☐
Winter Ascent: ☐☐☐☐☐
Trailhead: _____

Date:

Time:

Weather:

Companions:

Future Advice:

_____

_____

_____

_____

_____

_____

_____

_____

_____

_____

_____

An Socach
The snout (or projecting place)
(1069m)

Summer Ascent: ☐☐☐☐☐
Winter Ascent: ☐☐☐☐☐

Trailhead: _____

Hill #: 67

Region #: 12

Date:

Time:

Weather:

Companions:

Future Advice:

_____

_____

_____

_____

_____

_____

_____

_____

_____

_____

_____

_____

_____

Meall Corranaich

Notched hill (or prickly hill) (or rounded hill of lament-passion and sorrow)

(1069m)

Hill #: **68**

Region #: **02**

Summer Ascent: ☐☐☐☐☐
Winter Ascent: ☐☐☐☐☐

Trailhead: _____

Date:

Time:

Weather:

Companions:

Future Advice:

Glas Maol
Greenish-grey bare hill
(1068m)

Summer Ascent: ☐☐☐☐☐
Winter Ascent: ☐☐☐☐☐

Trailhead: _____

Hill #: 69

Region #: 07

Date:

Time:

Weather:

Companions:

Future Advice:

_____
_____
_____
_____
_____
_____
_____
_____
_____
_____
_____
_____
_____

Sgurr Fhuaran
Peak of the fountain/ spring (obscure)
(1067m)

Summer Ascent: ☐☐☐☐☐
Winter Ascent: ☐☐☐☐☐
Trailhead: _____

Date:

Time:

Weather:

Companions:

Future Advice:

_____

_____

_____

_____

_____

_____

_____

_____

_____

_____

_____

_____

_____

Cairn of Claise
Hill of the green grassy place
(1064m)

Summer Ascent: ☐☐☐☐☐
Winter Ascent: ☐☐☐☐☐

Trailhead: _____

Date:

Time:

Weather:

Companions:

Future Advice:

_____

_____

_____

_____

_____

_____

_____

_____

_____

_____

_____

Bidean a' Ghlas Thuill (An Teallach)

Peak of the greenish-grey hollow

(1062m)

Hill #: 72

Region #: 14

Summer Ascent: ☐☐☐☐☐
Winter Ascent: ☐☐☐☐☐
Trailhead: _____

Date:

Time:

Weather:

Companions:

Future Advice:

_____
_____
_____
_____
_____
_____
_____
_____
_____
_____
_____
_____
_____

Sgurr Fiona (An Teallach)
Light coloured peak (or peak of wine)
(1060m)

Summer Ascent: ☐☐☐☐☐
Winter Ascent: ☐☐☐☐☐

Trailhead: _____

Date:

Time:

Weather:

Companions:

Future Advice:

_____

_____

_____

_____

_____

_____

_____

_____

_____

_____

_____

_____

_____

_____

Na Gruagaichean
The maidens
(1056m)

Summer Ascent: ☐☐☐☐☐
Winter Ascent: ☐☐☐☐☐

Trailhead: _____

Date:

Time:

Weather:

Companions:

Future Advice:

Spidean a Choire Leith (Liathach)
Peak of the greyish corrie
(1055m)

Summer Ascent: ☐☐☐☐☐
Winter Ascent: ☐☐☐☐☐
Trailhead: _____

Hill #: **75**

Region #: **13**

Date:

Time:

Weather:

Companions:

Future Advice:

_____
_____
_____
_____
_____
_____
_____
_____
_____
_____
_____
_____
_____

Stob Poite Coire Ardair
Peak of the pot of the high corrie
(1054m)

Hill #: 76

Region #: 09

Summer Ascent: ☐☐☐☐☐
Winter Ascent: ☐☐☐☐☐
Trailhead: _____

Date:

Time:

Weather:

Companions:

Future Advice:

_____
_____
_____
_____
_____
_____
_____
_____
_____
_____
_____
_____
_____
_____

Toll Creagach
Rocky hollow
(1054m)

Summer Ascent: ☐☐☐☐☐
Winter Ascent: ☐☐☐☐☐

Trailhead: _____

Hill #: **77**

Region #: **11**

Date:

Time:

Weather:

Companions:

Future Advice:

_____

_____

_____

_____

_____

_____

_____

_____

_____

_____

_____

_____

_____

Sgurr a' Chaorachain
Peak of the little field of the berries (round berries)
(1053m)

Hill #: 78

Region #: 12

Summer Ascent: ☐☐☐☐☐
Winter Ascent: ☐☐☐☐☐

Trailhead: _____

Date:

Time:

Weather:

Companions:

Future Advice:

_____

_____

_____

_____

_____

_____

_____

_____

_____

_____

_____

Beinn a' Chaorainn
Hill of the rowan (trees)
(1052m)

Summer Ascent: ☐☐☐☐☐
Winter Ascent: ☐☐☐☐☐

Trailhead: _____

Hill #: 79

Region #: 09

Date:

Time:

Weather:

Companions:

Future Advice:

_____
_____
_____
_____
_____
_____
_____
_____
_____
_____
_____
_____
_____

Glas Tulaichean
Green-grey hills
(1051m)

Summer Ascent: ☐☐☐☐☐
Winter Ascent: ☐☐☐☐☐

Trailhead: _____

Date:

Time:

Weather:

Companions:

Future Advice:

_____

_____

_____

_____

_____

_____

_____

_____

_____

_____

_____

_____

Geal Charn
White hill
(1049m)

Summer Ascent: ☐☐☐☐☐
Winter Ascent: ☐☐☐☐☐

Trailhead: _____

Hill #: 81

Region #: 04

Date:

Time:

Weather:

Companions:

Future Advice:

_____

_____

_____

_____

_____

_____

_____

_____

_____

_____

_____

_____

_____

_____

Sgurr Fuar-thuill
Peak of the cold hollow
(1049m)

Hill #: 82

Region #: 12

Summer Ascent: ☐☐☐☐☐
Winter Ascent: ☐☐☐☐☐
Trailhead: _____

Date:

Time:

Weather:

Companions:

Future Advice:

Carn an t-Sagairt Mor
Big hill of the priest
(1047m)

Summer Ascent: ☐☐☐☐☐
Winter Ascent: ☐☐☐☐☐

Trailhead: _____

Hill #: 83

Region #: 07

Date:

Time:

Weather:

Companions:

Future Advice:

_____
_____
_____
_____
_____
_____
_____
_____
_____
_____
_____
_____

Creag Mhor
Big Creag (rock cliff)
(1047m)

Hill #: 84

Region #: 02

Summer Ascent: ☐☐☐☐☐
Winter Ascent: ☐☐☐☐☐
Trailhead: _____

Date:

Time:

Weather:

Companions:

Future Advice:

_____
_____
_____
_____
_____
_____
_____
_____
_____
_____
_____
_____

Ben Wyvis, Glas Leathad Mor
Awesome hill (or hill of terror)
(1046m)

Summer Ascent: ☐☐☐☐☐

Winter Ascent: ☐☐☐☐☐

Hill #: 85

Trailhead: _____

Region #: 15

Date:

Time:

Weather:

Companions:

Future Advice:

Chno Dearg
Red hill (or red nut)
(1046m)

Hill #: 86

Region #: 04

Summer Ascent: ☐☐☐☐☐
Winter Ascent: ☐☐☐☐☐

Trailhead: _____

Date:

Time:

Weather:

Companions:

Future Advice:

_____
_____
_____
_____
_____
_____
_____
_____
_____
_____
_____
_____
_____

Cruach Ardrain
Stack of the high part
(1046m)

Summer Ascent: ☐☐☐☐☐
Winter Ascent: ☐☐☐☐☐

Trailhead: _____

Hill #: 87

Region #: 01

Date:

Time:

Weather:

Companions:

Future Advice:

Beinn Iutharn Mhor
Big hill of the sharp ridge (or sharp edge)
(1045m)

Hill #: 88

Region #: 06

Summer Ascent: ☐☐☐☐☐
Winter Ascent: ☐☐☐☐☐
Trailhead: _____

Date:

Time:

Weather:

Companions:

Future Advice:

Meall nan Tarmachan
Hill of the ptarmigan (bird)
(1044m)

Summer Ascent: ☐☐☐☐☐
Winter Ascent: ☐☐☐☐☐

Trailhead: _____

Hill #: 89

Region #: 02

Date:

Time:

Weather:

Companions:

Future Advice:

Stob Coire 'an Albannaich
Peak of the Scotsman's corrie
(1044m)

Hill #: 90

Region #: 03

Summer Ascent: ☐☐☐☐☐
Winter Ascent: ☐☐☐☐☐
Trailhead: _____

Date:

Time:

Weather:

Companions:

Future Advice:

_____
_____
_____
_____
_____
_____
_____
_____
_____
_____
_____
_____

Carn Mairg
Hill of sorrow (or rusty red hill)
(1041m)

Summer Ascent: ☐☐☐☐☐
Winter Ascent: ☐☐☐☐☐

Trailhead: _____

Hill #: 91

Region #: 02

Date:

Time:

Weather:

Companions:

Future Advice:

_____
_____
_____
_____
_____
_____
_____
_____
_____
_____
_____
_____

Sgurr na Ciche
Peak of the breast
(1040m)

Hill #: 92

Region #: 10

Summer Ascent: ☐☐☐☐☐
Winter Ascent: ☐☐☐☐☐

Trailhead: _____

Date:

Time:

Weather:

Companions:

Future Advice:

_____
_____
_____
_____
_____
_____
_____
_____
_____
_____
_____

Meall Ghaordie
Rounded hill of the shoulder, arm, hand
(1039m)

Summer Ascent: ☐☐☐☐☐

Winter Ascent: ☐☐☐☐☐

Trailhead: _____

Hill #: 93

Region #: 02

Date:

Time:

Weather:

Companions:

Future Advice:

_____

_____

_____

_____

_____

_____

_____

_____

_____

_____

_____

_____

_____

Beinn Achaladair
Field of hard water
(1038m)

Hill #: **94**

Region #: **02**

Summer Ascent: ☐☐☐☐☐
Winter Ascent: ☐☐☐☐☐
Trailhead: _____

Date:

Time:

Weather:

Companions:

Future Advice:

_____

_____

_____

_____

_____

_____

_____

_____

_____

_____

_____

_____

Carn a' Mhaim

Hill of the pass (or cairn of the big rounded hill)
(1037m)

Summer Ascent: ☐☐☐☐☐

Winter Ascent: ☐☐☐☐☐

Hill #: 95

Region #: 08

Trailhead: _____

Date:

Time:

Weather:

Companions:

Future Advice:

_____

_____

_____

_____

_____

_____

_____

_____

_____

_____

_____

_____

_____

_____

Sgurr a' Bhealaich Dheirg
Peak of the red pass
(1036m)

Hill #: 96

Region #: 11

Summer Ascent: ☐☐☐☐☐
Winter Ascent: ☐☐☐☐☐

Trailhead: _____

Date:

Time:

Weather:

Companions:

Future Advice:

Gleouraich
Roaring noise
(1035m)

Summer Ascent: ☐☐☐☐☐

Winter Ascent: ☐☐☐☐☐

Trailhead: _____

Hill #: 97

Region #: 10

Date:

Time:

Weather:

Companions:

Future Advice:

_____

_____

_____

_____

_____

_____

_____

_____

_____

_____

_____

_____

_____

Carn Dearg
Red hill
(1034m)

Hill #: 98

Region #: 04

Summer Ascent: ☐☐☐☐☐
Winter Ascent: ☐☐☐☐☐
Trailhead: _____

Date:

Time:

Weather:

Companions:

Future Advice:

_____
_____
_____
_____
_____
_____
_____
_____
_____
_____
_____
_____
_____

Am Bodach
The old man
(1032m)

Summer Ascent: ☐☐☐☐☐
Winter Ascent: ☐☐☐☐☐

Trailhead: _____

Hill #: 99

Region #: 04

Date:

Time:

Weather:

Companions:

Future Advice:

_____

_____

_____

_____

_____

_____

_____

_____

_____

_____

_____

_____

_____

Beinn Fhada
Long hill
(1032m)

Hill #: 100

Region #: 11

Summer Ascent: ☐☐☐☐☐
Winter Ascent: ☐☐☐☐☐

Trailhead: _____

Date:

Time:

Weather:

Companions:

Future Advice:

_____
_____
_____
_____
_____
_____
_____
_____
_____
_____
_____
_____

Ben Oss
outlet hill (or elk hill)
(1029m)

Summer Ascent: ☐☐☐☐☐
Winter Ascent: ☐☐☐☐☐

Trailhead: _____

Hill #: **101**

Region #: **01**

Date:

Time:

Weather:

Companions:

Future Advice:

_____

_____

_____

_____

_____

_____

_____

_____

_____

_____

_____

_____

_____

Carn an Righ
Hill of the king
(1029m)

Summer Ascent: ☐☐☐☐☐
Winter Ascent: ☐☐☐☐☐

Trailhead: _____

Date:

Time:

Weather:

Companions:

Future Advice:

_____
_____
_____
_____
_____
_____
_____
_____
_____
_____
_____
_____

Carn Gorm
Blue hill
(1029m)

Summer Ascent: ☐☐☐☐☐
Winter Ascent: ☐☐☐☐☐

Trailhead: _____

Hill #: 103

Region #: 02

Date:

Time:

Weather:

Companions:

Future Advice:

_____
_____
_____
_____
_____
_____
_____
_____
_____
_____
_____
_____
_____
_____

Sgurr a' Mhaoraich
Peak of the shellfish
(1027m)

Hill #: 104

Region #: 10

Summer Ascent: ☐☐☐☐☐
Winter Ascent: ☐☐☐☐☐
Trailhead: _____

Date:

Time:

Weather:

Companions:

Future Advice:

_____
_____
_____
_____
_____
_____
_____
_____
_____
_____
_____
_____

Sgurr na Ciste Duibhe
Peak of the black chest (or coffin)
(1027m)

Summer Ascent: ☐☐☐☐☐

Winter Ascent: ☐☐☐☐☐

Trailhead: _____

Hill #: **105**

Region #: **11**

Date:

Time:

Weather:

Companions:

Future Advice:

Ben Challum
Malcolm's hill
(1025m)

Hill #: **106**

Region #: **02**

Summer Ascent: ☐☐☐☐☐
Winter Ascent: ☐☐☐☐☐
Trailhead: _____

Date:

Time:

Weather:

Companions:

Future Advice:

_____
_____
_____
_____
_____
_____
_____
_____
_____
_____
_____
_____

Sgorr Dhearg (Beinn a' Bheithir)
Red peak
(1024m)

Summer Ascent: ☐☐☐☐☐
Winter Ascent: ☐☐☐☐☐

Trailhead: _____

Date:

Time:

Weather:

Companions:

Future Advice:

Mullach an Rathain (Liathach)

Summit of the row of pinnacles

(1023m)

Hill #: **108**

Region #: **13**

Summer Ascent: ☐☐☐☐☐
Winter Ascent: ☐☐☐☐☐
Trailhead: _____

Date:

Time:

Weather:

Companions:

Future Advice:

_____

_____

_____

_____

_____

_____

_____

_____

_____

_____

_____

Aonach air Chrith
Trembling hill
(1021m)

Summer Ascent: ☐☐☐☐☐

Winter Ascent: ☐☐☐☐☐

Trailhead: _____

Hill #: 109

Region #: 10

Date:

Time:

Weather:

Companions:

Future Advice:

_____

_____

_____

_____

_____

_____

_____

_____

_____

_____

_____

_____

_____

_____

Buachaille Etive Mor (Stob Dearg)
"Big herdsman of Etive"– red peak
(1021m)

Hill #: **110**

Region #: **03**

Summer Ascent: ☐☐☐☐☐
Winter Ascent: ☐☐☐☐☐

Trailhead: _____

Date:

Time:

Weather:

Companions:

Future Advice:

Ladhar Bheinn
Hoof/ claw hill
(1020m)

Summer Ascent: ☐☐☐☐☐
Winter Ascent: ☐☐☐☐☐

Trailhead: _____

Hill #: **111**

Region #: **10**

Date:

Time:

Weather:

Companions:

Future Advice:

_____
_____
_____
_____
_____
_____
_____
_____
_____
_____
_____
_____
_____

Beinn Bheoil
Hill of the mouth (or fore hill)
(1019m)

Summer Ascent: ☐☐☐☐☐
Winter Ascent: ☐☐☐☐☐
Trailhead: _____

Date:

Time:

Weather:

Companions:

Future Advice:

_____
_____
_____
_____
_____
_____
_____
_____
_____
_____
_____
_____
_____

Carn an Tuirc
Hill of the boar
(1019m)

Summer Ascent: ☐☐☐☐☐
Winter Ascent: ☐☐☐☐☐

Trailhead: _____

Hill #: 113

Region #: 07

Date:

Time:

Weather:

Companions:

Future Advice:

Mullach Clach a' Bhlair
Summit of the stone of the plain
(1019m)

Hill #: **114**

Region #: **08**

Summer Ascent: ☐☐☐☐☐
Winter Ascent: ☐☐☐☐☐
Trailhead: _____

Date:

Time:

Weather:

Companions:

Future Advice:

_____
_____
_____
_____
_____
_____
_____
_____
_____
_____
_____
_____

Mullach Coire Mhic Fhearchair
Summit of the corrie of Farquhar's son
(1018m)

Summer Ascent: ☐☐☐☐☐

Winter Ascent: ☐☐☐☐☐

Trailhead: _____

Hill #: **115**

Region #: **14**

Date:

Time:

Weather:

Companions:

Future Advice:

_____

_____

_____

_____

_____

_____

_____

_____

_____

_____

_____

_____

_____

Garbh Chioch Mhor
Big rough place of the breast
(1013m)

Hill #: **116**

Region #: **10**

Summer Ascent: ☐☐☐☐☐
Winter Ascent: ☐☐☐☐☐
Trailhead: _____

Date:

Time:

Weather:

Companions:

Future Advice:

_____

_____

_____

_____

_____

_____

_____

_____

_____

_____

_____

_____

Cairn Bannoch
Hill of the point
(1012m)

Summer Ascent: ☐☐☐☐☐

Winter Ascent: ☐☐☐☐☐

Trailhead: _____

Hill #: 117

Region #: 07

Date:

Time:

Weather:

Companions:

Future Advice:

Beinn Udlamain
Gloomy mountain
(1011m)

Hill #: 118

Region #: 05

Summer Ascent: ☐☐☐☐☐
Winter Ascent: ☐☐☐☐☐
Trailhead: _____

Date:

Time:

Weather:

Companions:

Future Advice:

_____

_____

_____

_____

_____

_____

_____

_____

_____

_____

_____

_____

_____

Ben Ime
Butter hill
(1011m)

Summer Ascent: ☐☐☐☐☐

Winter Ascent: ☐☐☐☐☐

Trailhead: _____

Date:

Time:

Weather:

Companions:

Future Advice:

_____

_____

_____

_____

_____

_____

_____

_____

_____

_____

_____

_____

_____

_____

Beinn Eighe (Ruadh-stac Mor)
File hill (or big red peak)
(1010m)

Summer Ascent: ☐☐☐☐☐
Winter Ascent: ☐☐☐☐☐

Trailhead: _____

Date:

Time:

Weather:

Companions:

Future Advice:

_____

_____

_____

_____

_____

_____

_____

_____

_____

_____

_____

_____

_____

Sgurr an Doire Leathain
Peak of the broad thicket
(1010m)

Summer Ascent: ☐☐☐☐☐

Winter Ascent: ☐☐☐☐☐

Trailhead: _____

Date:

Time:

Weather:

Companions:

Future Advice:

Sgurr Eilde Mor
Big peak of the hind
(1010m)

Hill #: 122

Region #: 04

Summer Ascent: ☐☐☐☐☐
Winter Ascent: ☐☐☐☐☐
Trailhead: _____

Date:

Time:

Weather:

Companions:

Future Advice:

_____
_____
_____
_____
_____
_____
_____
_____
_____
_____
_____
_____

The Saddle
The Saddle
(1010m)

Summer Ascent: ☐☐☐☐☐
Winter Ascent: ☐☐☐☐☐

Trailhead: _____

Hill #: **123**

Region #: **10**

Date:

Time:

Weather:

Companions:

Future Advice:

_____

_____

_____

_____

_____

_____

_____

_____

_____

_____

_____

_____

_____

Beinn Dearg
Red hill
(1008m)

Hill #: 124

Region #: 06

Summer Ascent: ☐☐☐☐☐
Winter Ascent: ☐☐☐☐☐
Trailhead: _____

Date:

Time:

Weather:

Companions:

Future Advice:

_____
_____
_____
_____
_____
_____
_____
_____
_____
_____
_____
_____

An Sgarsoch
The place of the sharp rocks
(1006m)

Summer Ascent: ☐☐☐☐☐

Winter Ascent: ☐☐☐☐☐

Trailhead: _____

Hill #: 125

Region #: 06

Date:

Time:

Weather:

Companions:

Future Advice:

_____

_____

_____

_____

_____

_____

_____

_____

_____

_____

_____

_____

_____

_____

Carn Liath
Grey hill
(1006m)

Summer Ascent: ☐☐☐☐☐
Winter Ascent: ☐☐☐☐☐
Trailhead: _____

Date:

Time:

Weather:

Companions:

Future Advice:

_____
_____
_____
_____
_____
_____
_____
_____
_____
_____
_____
_____

Beinn Fhionnlaidh
Finlay's hill
(1005m)

Summer Ascent: ☐☐☐☐☐

Winter Ascent: ☐☐☐☐☐

Trailhead: _____

Hill #: 127

Region #: 11

Date:

Time:

Weather:

Companions:

Future Advice:

Maoile Lunndaidh
Bare hill of the wet place
(1005m)

Hill #: 128

Region #: 12

Summer Ascent: ☐☐☐☐☐
Winter Ascent: ☐☐☐☐☐
Trailhead: _____

Date:

Time:

Weather:

Companions:

Future Advice:

_____
_____
_____
_____
_____
_____
_____
_____
_____
_____
_____
_____

Beinn an Dothaidh
Hill of the scorching (or singeing)
(1004m)

Summer Ascent: ☐☐☐☐☐

Winter Ascent: ☐☐☐☐☐

Trailhead: _____

Hill #: 129

Region #: 02

Date:

Time:

Weather:

Companions:

Future Advice:

_____
_____
_____
_____
_____
_____
_____
_____
_____
_____
_____
_____
_____
_____

Sgurr an Lochain
Peak of the little loch
(1004m)

Summer Ascent: ☐☐☐☐☐
Winter Ascent: ☐☐☐☐☐
Trailhead: _____

Date: _____

Time: _____

Weather: _____

Companions: _____

Future Advice: _____

_____

_____

_____

_____

_____

_____

_____

_____

_____

_____

_____

_____

The Devil's Point
Penis of the demon
(1004m)

Summer Ascent: ☐☐☐☐☐
Winter Ascent: ☐☐☐☐☐

Trailhead: _____

Hill #: 131

Region #: 08

Date:

Time:

Weather:

Companions:

Future Advice:

_____

_____

_____

_____

_____

_____

_____

_____

_____

_____

_____

_____

_____

_____

Sgurr Mor
Big peak
(1003m)

Hill #: 132

Region #: 10

Summer Ascent: ☐☐☐☐☐
Winter Ascent: ☐☐☐☐☐
Trailhead: _____

Date:

Time:

Weather:

Companions:

Future Advice:

_____
_____
_____
_____
_____
_____
_____
_____
_____
_____
_____
_____
_____

Sail Chaorainn
Hill of the rowan
(1002m)

Summer Ascent: ☐☐☐☐☐
Winter Ascent: ☐☐☐☐☐

Trailhead: _____

Hill #: 133

Region #: 11

Date:

Time:

Weather:

Companions:

Future Advice:

_____
_____
_____
_____
_____
_____
_____
_____
_____
_____
_____
_____
_____

Sgurr na Carnach
Stony peak
(1002m)

Hill #: **134**

Region #: **11**

Summer Ascent: ☐☐☐☐☐
Winter Ascent: ☐☐☐☐☐
Trailhead: _____

Date:

Time:

Weather:

Companions:

Future Advice:

_____
_____
_____
_____
_____
_____
_____
_____
_____
_____
_____
_____

Aonach Mheadhoin
Middle hill (or middle ridge)
(1001m)

Summer Ascent: ☐☐☐☐☐

Winter Ascent: ☐☐☐☐☐

Trailhead: _____

Hill #: **135**

Region #: **11**

Date:

Time:

Weather:

Companions:

Future Advice:

_____

_____

_____

_____

_____

_____

_____

_____

_____

_____

_____

_____

_____

_____

Meall Greigh
Hill of horse studs
(1001m)

Hill #: **136**

Region #: **02**

Summer Ascent: ☐☐☐☐☐
Winter Ascent: ☐☐☐☐☐

Trailhead: _____

Date:

Time:

Weather:

Companions:

Future Advice:

_____

_____

_____

_____

_____

_____

_____

_____

_____

_____

_____

_____

Sgorr Dhonuill (Beinn a' Bheithir)
Donald's peak
(1001m)

Summer Ascent: ☐☐☐☐☐

Winter Ascent: ☐☐☐☐☐

Trailhead: _____

Hill #: 137

Region #: 03

Date:

Time:

Weather:

Companions:

Future Advice:

Sgurr Breac
Speckled peak
(999m)

Summer Ascent: ☐☐☐☐☐
Winter Ascent: ☐☐☐☐☐

Trailhead: _____

Date:

Time:

Weather:

Companions:

Future Advice:

_____
_____
_____
_____
_____
_____
_____
_____
_____
_____
_____
_____
_____

Sgurr Choinnich
Mossy peak
(999m)

Summer Ascent: ☐☐☐☐☐
Winter Ascent: ☐☐☐☐☐

Trailhead: _____

Date:

Time:

Weather:

Companions:

Future Advice:

_____

_____

_____

_____

_____

_____

_____

_____

_____

_____

_____

_____

_____

Stob Ban
White peak
(999m)

Summer Ascent: ☐☐☐☐☐
Winter Ascent: ☐☐☐☐☐
Trailhead: _____

Date:

Time:

Weather:

Companions:

Future Advice:

_____
_____
_____
_____
_____
_____
_____
_____
_____
_____
_____
_____
_____

Ben More Assynt
Big hill of Assynt (Norse: ass, a rocky ridge)
(998m)

Summer Ascent: ☐☐☐☐☐

Winter Ascent: ☐☐☐☐☐

Trailhead: _____

Hill #: 141

Region #: 16

Date:

Time:

Weather:

Companions:

Future Advice:

_____
_____
_____
_____
_____
_____
_____
_____
_____
_____
_____
_____
_____

Broad Cairn
Broad cairn (wide)
(998m)

Hill #: **142**

Region #: **07**

Summer Ascent: ☐☐☐☐☐
Winter Ascent: ☐☐☐☐☐

Trailhead: _____

Date:

Time:

Weather:

Companions:

Future Advice:

_____

_____

_____

_____

_____

_____

_____

_____

_____

_____

_____

_____

_____

Stob Diamh
Peak of the stag
(998m)

Summer Ascent: ☐☐☐☐☐

Winter Ascent: ☐☐☐☐☐

Hill #: **143**

Trailhead: _____

Region #: **03**

Date:

Time:

Weather:

Companions:

Future Advice:

_____
_____
_____
_____
_____
_____
_____
_____
_____
_____
_____
_____
_____

A' Chailleach
The old woman
(997m)

Summer Ascent: ☐☐☐☐☐
Winter Ascent: ☐☐☐☐☐

Trailhead: _____

Date:

Time:

Weather:

Companions:

Future Advice:

_____

_____

_____

_____

_____

_____

_____

_____

_____

_____

_____

Glas Bheinn Mhor
Big greenish-grey hill
(997m)

Summer Ascent: ☐☐☐☐☐
Winter Ascent: ☐☐☐☐☐

Trailhead: _____

Hill #: 145

Region #: 03

Date:

Time:

Weather:

Companions:

Future Advice:

_____
_____
_____
_____
_____
_____
_____
_____
_____
_____
_____
_____
_____
_____

Spidean Mialach
Peak of deer/other wild animals (or lousy peak)
(996m)

Summer Ascent: ☐☐☐☐☐
Winter Ascent: ☐☐☐☐☐

Trailhead: _____

Date:

Time:

Weather:

Companions:

Future Advice:

_____

_____

_____

_____

_____

_____

_____

_____

_____

_____

_____

An Caisteal
The castle
(995m)

Summer Ascent: ☐☐☐☐☐
Winter Ascent: ☐☐☐☐☐

Trailhead: _____

Date:

Time:

Weather:

Companions:

Future Advice:

_____

_____

_____

_____

_____

_____

_____

_____

_____

_____

_____

_____

Carn an Fhidhleir
Hill of the fiddler
(994m)

Hill #: **148**

Region #: **06**

Summer Ascent: ☐☐☐☐☐
Winter Ascent: ☐☐☐☐☐
Trailhead: _____

Date:

Time:

Weather:

Companions:

Future Advice:

_____
_____
_____
_____
_____
_____
_____
_____
_____
_____
_____
_____

Sgor na h-Ulaidh
Peak of the treasure
(994m)

Summer Ascent: ☐☐☐☐☐
Winter Ascent: ☐☐☐☐☐

Trailhead: _____

Hill #: 149

Region #: 03

Date:

Time:

Weather:

Companions:

Future Advice:

Sgurr na Ruaidhe
Peak of the redness
(993m)

Hill #: **150**

Region #: **12**

Summer Ascent: ☐☐☐☐☐
Winter Ascent: ☐☐☐☐☐

Trailhead: _____

Date:

Time:

Weather:

Companions:

Future Advice:

_____
_____
_____
_____
_____
_____
_____
_____
_____
_____
_____
_____
_____

Spidean Coire nan Clach (Beinn Eighe)
Peak of the stony corrie
(993m)

Summer Ascent: ☐☐☐☐☐
Winter Ascent: ☐☐☐☐☐

Trailhead: _____

Hill #: **151**

Region #: **13**

Date:

Time:

Weather:

Companions:

Future Advice:

_____

_____

_____

_____

_____

_____

_____

_____

_____

_____

_____

Carn nan Gobhar (Glen Cannich)
Hill of the goats
(992m)

Hill #: **152**

Region #: **12**

Summer Ascent: ☐☐☐☐☐
Winter Ascent: ☐☐☐☐☐
Trailhead: _____

Date:

Time:

Weather:

Companions:

Future Advice:

_____
_____
_____
_____
_____
_____
_____
_____
_____
_____
_____
_____

Carn nan Gobhar (Glen Strathfarrar)
Hill of the goats
(992m)

Summer Ascent: ☐☐☐☐☐

Winter Ascent: ☐☐☐☐☐

Hill #: 153

Trailhead: _____

Region #: 12

Date:

Time:

Weather:

Companions:

Future Advice:

_____

_____

_____

_____

_____

_____

_____

_____

_____

_____

_____

_____

_____

Sgurr Alasdair
Alexander's peak (Sherriff Alexander Nicholson)
(992m)

Hill #: **154**

Region #: **17**

Summer Ascent: ☐☐☐☐☐
Winter Ascent: ☐☐☐☐☐
Trailhead: _____

Date:

Time:

Weather:

Companions:

Future Advice:

_____
_____
_____
_____
_____
_____
_____
_____
_____
_____
_____

Sgairneach Mhor
Big stony hillside (big scree)
(991m)

Summer Ascent: ☐☐☐☐☐
Winter Ascent: ☐☐☐☐☐

Trailhead: _____

Hill #: 155

Region #: 05

Date:

Time:

Weather:

Companions:

Future Advice:

_____
_____
_____
_____
_____
_____
_____
_____
_____
_____
_____
_____

Beinn Eunaich
Fowling hill
(989m)

Hill #: **156**

Region #: **03**

Summer Ascent: ☐☐☐☐☐
Winter Ascent: ☐☐☐☐☐
Trailhead: _____

Date:

Time:

Weather:

Companions:

Future Advice:

_____
_____
_____
_____
_____
_____
_____
_____
_____
_____
_____
_____

Sgurr Ban (Letterewe)
White peak
(989m)

Summer Ascent: ☐☐☐☐☐
Winter Ascent: ☐☐☐☐☐

Trailhead: _____

Hill #: 157

Region #: 14

Date:

Time:

Weather:

Companions:

Future Advice:

_____

_____

_____

_____

_____

_____

_____

_____

_____

_____

_____

_____

_____

Conival
Hill of the dog (or hill of the meeting)
(987m)

Hill #: **158**

Region #: **16**

Summer Ascent: ☐☐☐☐☐
Winter Ascent: ☐☐☐☐☐
Trailhead: _____

Date:

Time:

Weather:

Companions:

Future Advice:

_____

_____

_____

_____

_____

_____

_____

_____

_____

_____

_____

Creag Leachach
Slabby rock (creag)
(987m)

Summer Ascent: ☐☐☐☐☐

Winter Ascent: ☐☐☐☐☐

Hill #: 159

Trailhead: _____

Region #: 07

Date:

Time:

Weather:

Companions:

Future Advice:

_____

_____

_____

_____

_____

_____

_____

_____

_____

_____

_____

_____

_____

Druim Shionnach
Ridge of the fox
(987m)

Hill #: **160**

Region #: **10**

Summer Ascent: ☐☐☐☐☐
Winter Ascent: ☐☐☐☐☐
Trailhead: _____

Date:

Time:

Weather:

Companions:

Future Advice:

_____

_____

_____

_____

_____

_____

_____

_____

_____

_____

_____

_____

Gulvain
Gaelic gaorr (filth) or gaoir (noise)
(987m)

Summer Ascent: ☐☐☐☐☐

Winter Ascent: ☐☐☐☐☐

Trailhead: _____

Date:

Time:

Weather:

Companions:

Future Advice:

_____
_____
_____
_____
_____
_____
_____
_____
_____
_____
_____
_____
_____

Lurg Mhor
Big ridge stretching into the plain
(986m)

Hill #: **162**

Region #: **12**

Summer Ascent: ☐☐☐☐☐
Winter Ascent: ☐☐☐☐☐

Trailhead: _____

Date:

Time:

Weather:

Companions:

Future Advice:

_____
_____
_____
_____
_____
_____
_____
_____
_____
_____
_____
_____

Sgurr Dearg
(The Inaccessible Pinnacle)
Red peak
(986m)

Summer Ascent: ☐☐☐☐☐

Winter Ascent: ☐☐☐☐☐

Hill #: 163

Trailhead: _____

Region #: 17

Date:

Time:

Weather:

Companions:

Future Advice:

_____

_____

_____

_____

_____

_____

_____

_____

_____

_____

_____

_____

Sgurr Mhor (Beinn Alligin)
Jewelled hill
(986m)

Hill #: **164**

Region #: **13**

Summer Ascent: ☐☐☐☐☐
Winter Ascent: ☐☐☐☐☐
Trailhead: _____

Date:

Time:

Weather:

Companions:

Future Advice:

_____

_____

_____

_____

_____

_____

_____

_____

_____

_____

_____

Ben Vorlich (by Loch Earn)
Hill of the bay
(985m)

Summer Ascent: ☐☐☐☐☐

Winter Ascent: ☐☐☐☐☐

Trailhead: _____

Hill #: 165

Region #: 01

Date:

Time:

Weather:

Companions:

Future Advice:

An Gearanach
The complainer
(982m)

Summer Ascent: ☐☐☐☐☐
Winter Ascent: ☐☐☐☐☐

Trailhead: _____

Date:

Time:

Weather:

Companions:

Future Advice:

_____
_____
_____
_____
_____
_____
_____
_____
_____
_____
_____
_____
_____

Mullach na Dheiragain
Perhaps summit of the hawk (or of the kestrel)
(982m)

Summer Ascent: ☐☐☐☐☐

Winter Ascent: ☐☐☐☐☐

Trailhead: _____

Hill #: 167

Region #: 11

Date:

Time:

Weather:

Companions:

Future Advice:

_____

_____

_____

_____

_____

_____

_____

_____

_____

_____

_____

_____

_____

Maol Chinn-dearg
Bald red head
(981m)

Hill #: **168**

Region #: **10**

Summer Ascent: ☐☐☐☐☐
Winter Ascent: ☐☐☐☐☐
Trailhead: _____

Date:

Time:

Weather:

Companions:

Future Advice:

_____

_____

_____

_____

_____

_____

_____

_____

_____

_____

_____

_____

Meall nan Aighean
Big rock
(981m)

Summer Ascent: ☐☐☐☐☐
Winter Ascent: ☐☐☐☐☐
Trailhead: _____

Hill #: 169

Region #: 02

Date:

Time:

Weather:

Companions:

Future Advice:

_____
_____
_____
_____
_____
_____
_____
_____
_____
_____
_____
_____
_____
_____

Slioch - North Top
Spear
(981m)

Summer Ascent: ☐☐☐☐☐
Winter Ascent: ☐☐☐☐☐

Trailhead: _____

Date:

Time:

Weather:

Companions:

Future Advice:

_____

_____

_____

_____

_____

_____

_____

_____

_____

_____

_____

Stob Coire a' Chairn
Peak of the corrie of the cairn
(981m)

Summer Ascent: ☐☐☐☐☐

Winter Ascent: ☐☐☐☐☐

Trailhead: _____

Hill #: 171

Region #: 04

Date:

Time:

Weather:

Companions:

Future Advice:

_____
_____
_____
_____
_____
_____
_____
_____
_____
_____
_____
_____
_____

Beinn a' Chochuill
Hill of the hood or shell
(980m)

Hill #: **172**

Region #: **03**

Summer Ascent: ☐☐☐☐☐
Winter Ascent: ☐☐☐☐☐
Trailhead: _____

Date:

Time:

Weather:

Companions:

Future Advice:

_____
_____
_____
_____
_____
_____
_____
_____
_____
_____
_____
_____

Ciste Dhubh
Black chest (or dark coffin)
(979m)

Summer Ascent: ☐☐☐☐☐
Winter Ascent: ☐☐☐☐☐
Trailhead: _____

Hill #: **173**

Region #: **11**

Date:

Time:

Weather:

Companions:

Future Advice:

_____
_____
_____
_____
_____
_____
_____
_____
_____
_____
_____
_____

Stob Coire Sgriodain
Peak of the corrie of the scree
(979m)

Hill #: **174**

Region #: **04**

Summer Ascent: ☐☐☐☐☐
Winter Ascent: ☐☐☐☐☐
Trailhead: _____

Date:

Time:

Weather:

Companions:

Future Advice:

_____
_____
_____
_____
_____
_____
_____
_____
_____
_____
_____
_____

Beinn Dubhchraig
Black-rock hill
(978m)

Summer Ascent: ☐☐☐☐☐
Winter Ascent: ☐☐☐☐☐
Trailhead: _____

Hill #: **175**

Region #: **01**

Date:

Time:

Weather:

Companions:

Future Advice:

_____
_____
_____
_____
_____
_____
_____
_____
_____
_____
_____
_____

Cona' Mheall
Hill of the dog (or hill of the meeting)
(978m)

Summer Ascent: ☐☐☐☐☐
Winter Ascent: ☐☐☐☐☐

Trailhead: _____

Date:

Time:

Weather:

Companions:

Future Advice:

_____

_____

_____

_____

_____

_____

_____

_____

_____

_____

_____

Meall nan Ceapraichean
Hill of the Backs (or hilllocks)
(977m)

Summer Ascent: ☐☐☐☐☐
Winter Ascent: ☐☐☐☐☐

Trailhead: _____

Hill #: 177

Region #: 15

Date:

Time:

Weather:

Companions:

Future Advice:

Stob Ban
White peak
(977m)

Summer Ascent: ☐☐☐☐☐
Winter Ascent: ☐☐☐☐☐
Trailhead: _____

Date:

Time:

Weather:

Companions:

Future Advice:

_____

_____

_____

_____

_____

_____

_____

_____

_____

_____

_____

_____

A' Mharconaich
The horse place
(975m)

Summer Ascent: ☐☐☐☐☐
Winter Ascent: ☐☐☐☐☐

Trailhead: _____

Hill #: 179

Region #: 05

Date:

Time:

Weather:

Companions:

Future Advice:

_____
_____
_____
_____
_____
_____
_____
_____
_____
_____
_____
_____
_____

Carn a' Gheoidh
Hill of the goose
(975m)

Hill #: **180**

Region #: **06**

Summer Ascent: ☐☐☐☐☐
Winter Ascent: ☐☐☐☐☐

Trailhead: _____

Date:

Time:

Weather:

Companions:

Future Advice:

_____

_____

_____

_____

_____

_____

_____

_____

_____

_____

_____

_____

Carn Liath
Grey hill
(975m)

Summer Ascent: ☐☐☐☐☐
Winter Ascent: ☐☐☐☐☐

Trailhead: _____

Hill #: **181**

Region #: **06**

Date:

Time:

Weather:

Companions:

Future Advice:

_____
_____
_____
_____
_____
_____
_____
_____
_____
_____
_____
_____
_____

Stuc a' Chroin
Peak of harm/danger (or peak of the sheep fold)
(975m)

Hill #: 182

Region #: 01

Summer Ascent: ☐☐☐☐☐
Winter Ascent: ☐☐☐☐☐
Trailhead: _____

Date:

Time:

Weather:

Companions:

Future Advice:

_____
_____
_____
_____
_____
_____
_____
_____
_____
_____
_____
_____

Beinn Sgritheall
Scree or gravel hill
(974m)

Summer Ascent: ☐☐☐☐☐

Winter Ascent: ☐☐☐☐☐

Trailhead: _____

Hill #: **183**

Region #: **10**

Date:

Time:

Weather:

Companions:

Future Advice:

Ben Lomond
Beacon hill
(974m)

Hill #: **184**

Region #: **01**

Summer Ascent: ☐☐☐☐☐
Winter Ascent: ☐☐☐☐☐

Trailhead: _____

Date:

Time:

Weather:

Companions:

Future Advice:

_____
_____
_____
_____
_____
_____
_____
_____
_____
_____
_____
_____

Sgurr a' Ghreadhaidh
Peak of torment/anxiety (or peak of whipping)
(973m)

Summer Ascent: ☐☐☐☐☐

Winter Ascent: ☐☐☐☐☐

Trailhead: _____

Hill #: **185**

Region #: **17**

Date:

Time:

Weather:

Companions:

Future Advice:

213

Meall Garbh
Rough hill
(968m)

Hill #: 186

Region #: 02

Summer Ascent: ☐☐☐☐☐
Winter Ascent: ☐☐☐☐☐
Trailhead: _____

Date:

Time:

Weather:

Companions:

Future Advice:

_____
_____
_____
_____
_____
_____
_____
_____
_____
_____
_____
_____
_____

A' Mhaighdean
The maiden
(967m)

Summer Ascent: ☐☐☐☐☐
Winter Ascent: ☐☐☐☐☐

Hill #: 187

Trailhead: _____

Region #: 14

Date:

Time:

Weather:

Companions:

Future Advice:

_____
_____
_____
_____
_____
_____
_____
_____
_____
_____
_____
_____
_____
_____

Sgorr nam Fiannaidh (Aonach Eagach)
Peak of the Fian warriors
(967m)

Hill #: **188**

Region #: **03**

Summer Ascent: ☐☐☐☐☐
Winter Ascent: ☐☐☐☐☐
Trailhead: _____

Date:

Time:

Weather:

Companions:

Future Advice:

_____
_____
_____
_____
_____
_____
_____
_____
_____
_____
_____
_____

Ben More
Big hill
(966m)

Summer Ascent: ☐☐☐☐☐

Winter Ascent: ☐☐☐☐☐

Trailhead: _____

Hill #: 189

Region #: 17

Date:

Time:

Weather:

Companions:

Future Advice:

_____

_____

_____

_____

_____

_____

_____

_____

_____

_____

_____

_____

Sgurr na Banachdich
Milk maid's peak (or smallpox peak)
(965m)

Hill #: **190**

Region #: **17**

Summer Ascent: ☐☐☐☐☐
Winter Ascent: ☐☐☐☐☐

Trailhead: _____

Date:

Time:

Weather:

Companions:

Future Advice:

_____

_____

_____

_____

_____

_____

_____

_____

_____

_____

_____

_____

Sgurr nan Gillean
Peak of the young men (or peak of the gullies)
(964m)

Summer Ascent: ☐☐☐☐☐
Winter Ascent: ☐☐☐☐☐

Hill #: **191**

Region #: **17**

Trailhead: _____

Date:

Time:

Weather:

Companions:

Future Advice:

_____

_____

_____

_____

_____

_____

_____

_____

_____

_____

_____

_____

_____

Carn a' Chlamain
Hill of the kite/ buzzard (or of the kite)
(963m)

Hill #: 192

Region #: 06

Summer Ascent: ☐☐☐☐☐
Winter Ascent: ☐☐☐☐☐
Trailhead: _____

Date:

Time:

Weather:

Companions:

Future Advice:

_____
_____
_____
_____
_____
_____
_____
_____
_____
_____
_____
_____
_____

Sgurr Thuilm
Peak of the rounded hillock
(963m)

Summer Ascent: ☐☐☐☐☐

Winter Ascent: ☐☐☐☐☐

Trailhead: _____

Hill #: **193**

Region #: **10**

Date:

Time:

Weather:

Companions:

Future Advice:

_____

_____

_____

_____

_____

_____

_____

_____

_____

_____

_____

_____

Ben Klibreck
Hill of the speckled cliff/slope
(962m)

Hill #: **194**

Region #: **16**

Summer Ascent: ☐☐☐☐☐
Winter Ascent: ☐☐☐☐☐

Trailhead: _____

Date:

Time:

Weather:

Companions:

Future Advice:

_____

_____

_____

_____

_____

_____

_____

_____

_____

_____

_____

_____

_____

Sgorr Ruadh
Red peak
(962m)

Summer Ascent: ☐☐☐☐☐

Winter Ascent: ☐☐☐☐☐

Trailhead: _____

Hill #: **195**

Region #: **13**

Date:

Time:

Weather:

Companions:

Future Advice:

Beinn nan Aighenan
Hill of the hinds
(960m)

Hill #: **196**

Region #: **03**

Summer Ascent: ☐☐☐☐☐
Winter Ascent: ☐☐☐☐☐

Trailhead: _____

Date:

Time:

Weather:

Companions:

Future Advice:

_____
_____
_____
_____
_____
_____
_____
_____
_____
_____
_____
_____

Stuchd an Lochain
Peak of the little loch
(960m)

Summer Ascent: ☐☐☐☐☐
Winter Ascent: ☐☐☐☐☐

Trailhead: _____

Hill #: 197

Region #: 02

Date:

Time:

Weather:

Companions:

Future Advice:

_____
_____
_____
_____
_____
_____
_____
_____
_____
_____
_____
_____
_____
_____

Beinn Fhionnlaidh
Finlay's hill
(959m)

Summer Ascent: ☐☐☐☐☐
Winter Ascent: ☐☐☐☐☐

Trailhead: _____

Date:

Time:

Weather:

Companions:

Future Advice:

_____
_____
_____
_____
_____
_____
_____
_____
_____
_____
_____

Meall Glas
Greenish-grey hill
(959m)

Summer Ascent: ☐☐☐☐☐

Winter Ascent: ☐☐☐☐☐

Trailhead: _____

Hill #: **199**

Region #: **02**

Date:

Time:

Weather:

Companions:

Future Advice:

Bruach na Frithe
Slope of the deer forest (or of the wild forest)
(958m)

Hill #: 200

Region #: 17

Summer Ascent: ☐☐☐☐☐
Winter Ascent: ☐☐☐☐☐
Trailhead: _____

Date:

Time:

Weather:

Companions:

Future Advice:

_____

_____

_____

_____

_____

_____

_____

_____

_____

_____

_____

Buachaille Etive Beag (Stob Dubh)
Small herdsman of Etive, black peak
(958m)

Summer Ascent: ☐☐☐☐☐

Winter Ascent: ☐☐☐☐☐

Hill #: 201

Trailhead: _____

Region #: 03

Date:

Time:

Weather:

Companions:

Future Advice:

_____

_____

_____

_____

_____

_____

_____

_____

_____

_____

_____

_____

_____

Tolmount
Doll mounth or hill (leading to Glen Doll)
(958m)

Hill #: 202

Region #: 07

Summer Ascent: ☐☐☐☐☐
Winter Ascent: ☐☐☐☐☐
Trailhead: _____

Date:

Time:

Weather:

Companions:

Future Advice:

_____
_____
_____
_____
_____
_____
_____
_____
_____
_____
_____
_____
_____

Carn Ghluasaid

Hill of movement (carn of movement)
(957m)

Summer Ascent: ☐☐☐☐☐

Winter Ascent: ☐☐☐☐☐

Trailhead: _____

Hill #: 203

Region #: 11

Date:

Time:

Weather:

Companions:

Future Advice:

Tom Buidhe
Yellow hill
(957m)

Hill #: 204

Region #: 07

Summer Ascent: ☐☐☐☐☐
Winter Ascent: ☐☐☐☐☐

Trailhead: _____

Date:

Time:

Weather:

Companions:

Future Advice:

_____
_____
_____
_____
_____
_____
_____
_____
_____
_____
_____
_____

Buachaille Etive Mor (Stob na Broige)
Peak of the sohe (shoe)
(956m)

Summer Ascent: ☐☐☐☐☐
Winter Ascent: ☐☐☐☐☐

Trailhead: _____

Hill #: 205

Region #: 03

Date:

Time:

Weather:

Companions:

Future Advice:

_____
_____
_____
_____
_____
_____
_____
_____
_____
_____
_____

Saileag
Little heel
(956m)

Hill #: **206**

Region #: **11**

Summer Ascent: ☐☐☐☐☐
Winter Ascent: ☐☐☐☐☐
Trailhead: _____

Date:

Time:

Weather:

Companions:

Future Advice:

_____
_____
_____
_____
_____
_____
_____
_____
_____
_____
_____
_____
_____

Sgurr nan Coireachean
Peak of the corries
(956m)

Summer Ascent: ☐☐☐☐☐
Winter Ascent: ☐☐☐☐☐

Trailhead: _____

Hill #: 207

Region #: 10

Date:

Time:

Weather:

Companions:

Future Advice:

_____

_____

_____

_____

_____

_____

_____

_____

_____

_____

_____

_____

Sgor Gaibhre
Goat's peak
(955m)

Summer Ascent: ☐☐☐☐☐
Winter Ascent: ☐☐☐☐☐
Trailhead: _____

Date:

Time:

Weather:

Companions:

Future Advice:

_____
_____
_____
_____
_____
_____
_____
_____
_____
_____
_____
_____

Beinn Liath Mhor Fannaich
Big grey hill of Fannich
(954m)

Summer Ascent: ☐☐☐☐☐

Winter Ascent: ☐☐☐☐☐

Hill #: 209

Trailhead: _____

Region #: 14

Date:

Time:

Weather:

Companions:

Future Advice:

_____

_____

_____

_____

_____

_____

_____

_____

_____

_____

_____

_____

_____

Am Faochagach
The place of the shells (or heathery place)
(953m)

Hill #: **210**

Region #: **15**

Summer Ascent: ☐☐☐☐☐
Winter Ascent: ☐☐☐☐☐
Trailhead: _____

Date:

Time:

Weather:

Companions:

Future Advice:

_____

_____

_____

_____

_____

_____

_____

_____

_____

_____

_____

_____

Beinn Mhanach
Monk hill
(953m)

Summer Ascent: ☐☐☐☐☐
Winter Ascent: ☐☐☐☐☐

Trailhead: _____

Hill #: **211**

Region #: **02**

Date:

Time:

Weather:

Companions:

Future Advice:

_____

_____

_____

_____

_____

_____

_____

_____

_____

_____

_____

_____

_____

Meall Dearg (Aonach Eagach)
Red hill
(953m)

Hill #: 212

Region #: 03

Summer Ascent: ☐☐☐☐☐
Winter Ascent: ☐☐☐☐☐

Trailhead: _____

Date:

Time:

Weather:

Companions:

Future Advice:

_____
_____
_____
_____
_____
_____
_____
_____
_____
_____
_____
_____

Sgurr nan Coireachan
Peak of the corries
(953m)

Summer Ascent: ☐☐☐☐☐
Winter Ascent: ☐☐☐☐☐

Hill #: 213

Region #: 10

Trailhead: _____

Date:

Time:

Weather:

Companions:

Future Advice:

_____
_____
_____
_____
_____
_____
_____
_____
_____
_____
_____
_____

Meall Chuaich
Hill of the quaich
(951m)

Hill #: 214

Region #: 05

Summer Ascent: ☐☐☐☐☐
Winter Ascent: ☐☐☐☐☐
Trailhead: _____

Date:

Time:

Weather:

Companions:

Future Advice:

_____
_____
_____
_____
_____
_____
_____
_____
_____
_____
_____
_____

Meall Gorm
Blue hill
(949m)

Summer Ascent: ☐☐☐☐☐
Winter Ascent: ☐☐☐☐☐

Trailhead: _____

Hill #: **215**

Region #: **14**

Date:

Time:

Weather:

Companions:

Future Advice:

_____
_____
_____
_____
_____
_____
_____
_____
_____
_____
_____
_____
_____
_____

Beinn Bhuidhe
Yellow hill
(948m)

Hill #: 216

Region #: 01

Summer Ascent: ☐☐☐☐☐
Winter Ascent: ☐☐☐☐☐

Trailhead: _____

Date:

Time:

Weather:

Companions:

Future Advice:

_____
_____
_____
_____
_____
_____
_____
_____
_____
_____
_____

Sgurr Mhic Choinnich
MacKenzie's peak (John MacKenzie, Cuillin guide)
(948m)

Summer Ascent: ☐☐☐☐☐

Winter Ascent: ☐☐☐☐☐

Trailhead: _____

Hill #: **217**

Region #: **17**

Date:

Time:

Weather:

Companions:

Future Advice:

_____

_____

_____

_____

_____

_____

_____

_____

_____

_____

_____

_____

Creag a' Mhaim
Rock of the large rounded hill
(947m)

Hill #: **218**

Region #: **10**

Summer Ascent: ☐☐☐☐☐
Winter Ascent: ☐☐☐☐☐
Trailhead: _____

Date:

Time:

Weather:

Companions:

Future Advice:

_____
_____
_____
_____
_____
_____
_____
_____
_____
_____
_____
_____

Driesh
Thorn bush (or bramble)
(947m)

Summer Ascent: ☐☐☐☐☐
Winter Ascent: ☐☐☐☐☐

Trailhead: _____

Hill #: 219

Region #: 07

Date:

Time:

Weather:

Companions:

Future Advice:

_____
_____
_____
_____
_____
_____
_____
_____
_____
_____
_____
_____
_____

Beinn Tulaichean
Hill of the hillocks
(946m)

Summer Ascent: ☐☐☐☐☐
Winter Ascent: ☐☐☐☐☐
Trailhead: _____

Date:

Time:

Weather:

Companions:

Future Advice:

_____
_____
_____
_____
_____
_____
_____
_____
_____
_____
_____

Carn Bhac
Hill of peat-banks
(946m)

Summer Ascent: ☐☐☐☐☐

Winter Ascent: ☐☐☐☐☐

Trailhead: _____

Hill #: 221

Region #: 06

Date:

Time:

Weather:

Companions:

Future Advice:

_____

_____

_____

_____

_____

_____

_____

_____

_____

_____

_____

_____

_____

_____

Meall Buidhe
Yellow hill
(946m)

Summer Ascent: ☐☐☐☐☐
Winter Ascent: ☐☐☐☐☐

Trailhead: _____

Date:

Time:

Weather:

Companions:

Future Advice:

_____
_____
_____
_____
_____
_____
_____
_____
_____
_____
_____
_____

Sgurr na Sgine
Peak of the knife
(946m)

Summer Ascent: ☐☐☐☐☐
Winter Ascent: ☐☐☐☐☐
Trailhead: _____

Hill #: 223

Region #: 10

Date:

Time:

Weather:

Companions:

Future Advice:

_____
_____
_____
_____
_____
_____
_____
_____
_____
_____
_____

Bidean a' Choire Sheasgaich
Peak of the corrie of the farrow cattle (milkless)
(945m)

Hill #: **224**

Region #: **12**

Summer Ascent: ☐☐☐☐☐
Winter Ascent: ☐☐☐☐☐
Trailhead: _____

Date:

Time:

Weather:

Companions:

Future Advice:

_____

_____

_____

_____

_____

_____

_____

_____

_____

_____

_____

Carn Dearg
Red hill
(945m)

Summer Ascent: ☐☐☐☐☐
Winter Ascent: ☐☐☐☐☐

Trailhead: _____

Date:

Time:

Weather:

Companions:

Future Advice:

_____

_____

_____

_____

_____

_____

_____

_____

_____

_____

Stob a' Choire Odhair
Peak of the dun-coloured corrie (or of the speckled corrie)
(945m)

Summer Ascent: ☐☐☐☐☐
Winter Ascent: ☐☐☐☐☐

Trailhead: _____

Date:

Time:

Weather:

Companions:

Future Advice:

_____
_____
_____
_____
_____
_____
_____
_____
_____
_____
_____

An Socach
The projecting place (beak or snout)
(944m)

Summer Ascent: ☐☐☐☐☐
Winter Ascent: ☐☐☐☐☐

Trailhead: _____

Hill #: 227

Region #: 06

Date:

Time:

Weather:

Companions:

Future Advice:

_____
_____
_____
_____
_____
_____
_____
_____
_____
_____
_____
_____
_____

Sgurr Dubh Mor
Big black peak
(944m)

Hill #: 228

Region #: 17

Summer Ascent: ☐☐☐☐☐
Winter Ascent: ☐☐☐☐☐

Trailhead: _____

Date:

Time:

Weather:

Companions:

Future Advice:

_____
_____
_____
_____
_____
_____
_____
_____
_____
_____
_____
_____

Ben Vorlich
Hill of the bay
(943m)

Summer Ascent: ☐☐☐☐☐
Winter Ascent: ☐☐☐☐☐

Hill #: **229**

Trailhead: _____

Region #: **01**

Date:

Time:

Weather:

Companions:

Future Advice:

_____
_____
_____
_____
_____
_____
_____
_____
_____
_____
_____
_____
_____
_____

Binnean Beag
Small peak
(943m)

Summer Ascent: ☐☐☐☐☐
Winter Ascent: ☐☐☐☐☐
Trailhead: _____

Date:

Time:

Weather:

Companions:

Future Advice:

_____
_____
_____
_____
_____
_____
_____
_____
_____
_____
_____
_____

Beinn a' Chroin
Hill of harm or danger (or of the sheepfold)
(942m)

Summer Ascent: ☐☐☐☐☐

Winter Ascent: ☐☐☐☐☐

Trailhead: _____

Hill #: 231

Region #: 01

Date:

Time:

Weather:

Companions:

Future Advice:

_____

_____

_____

_____

_____

_____

_____

_____

_____

_____

_____

_____

_____

Carn Dearg
Red hill
(941m)

Hill #: 232

Region #: 04

Summer Ascent: ☐☐☐☐☐
Winter Ascent: ☐☐☐☐☐

Trailhead: _____

Date:

Time:

Weather:

Companions:

Future Advice:

_____
_____
_____
_____
_____
_____
_____
_____
_____
_____
_____
_____

Carn na Caim
Cairn of the curve
(941m)

Summer Ascent: ☐☐☐☐☐
Winter Ascent: ☐☐☐☐☐

Trailhead: _____

Hill #: **233**

Region #: **05**

Date:

Time:

Weather:

Companions:

Future Advice:

_____

_____

_____

_____

_____

_____

_____

_____

_____

_____

_____

_____

Luinne Bheinne

Hill of anger (or hill of mirth/ melody) (or sea swelling hill)

(939m)

Hill #: **234**

Region #: **10**

Summer Ascent: ☐☐☐☐☐
Winter Ascent: ☐☐☐☐☐

Trailhead: _____

Date:

Time:

Weather:

Companions:

Future Advice:

_____

_____

_____

_____

_____

_____

_____

_____

_____

_____

_____

Mount Keen
Gaelic monadh, meaning hill (or smooth gentle hill)
(939m)

Summer Ascent: ☐☐☐☐☐

Winter Ascent: ☐☐☐☐☐

Trailhead: _____

Date:

Time:

Weather:

Companions:

Future Advice:

_____

_____

_____

_____

_____

_____

_____

_____

_____

_____

_____

_____

_____

_____

_____

_____

Mullach na Coirean
Summit of the corries
(939m)

Hill #: 236

Region #: 04

Summer Ascent: ☐☐☐☐☐
Winter Ascent: ☐☐☐☐☐
Trailhead: _____

Date:

Time:

Weather:

Companions:

Future Advice:

_____
_____
_____
_____
_____
_____
_____
_____
_____
_____
_____
_____

Beinn Sgulaird
Hat-shaped hill?
(937m)

Summer Ascent: ☐☐☐☐☐

Winter Ascent: ☐☐☐☐☐

Trailhead: _____

Date:

Time:

Weather:

Companions:

Future Advice:

Beinn Tarsuinn
Transverse hill
(937m)

Hill #: 238

Region #: 14

Summer Ascent: ☐☐☐☐☐
Winter Ascent: ☐☐☐☐☐

Trailhead: _____

Date:

Time:

Weather:

Companions:

Future Advice:

_____
_____
_____
_____
_____
_____
_____
_____
_____
_____
_____
_____
_____

Sron a' Choire Ghairbh
Nose of the rough corrie
(937m)

Summer Ascent: ☐☐☐☐☐
Winter Ascent: ☐☐☐☐☐

Trailhead: _____

Hill #: 239

Region #: 10

Date:

Time:

Weather:

Companions:

Future Advice:

_____

_____

_____

_____

_____

_____

_____

_____

_____

_____

_____

A' Bhuidheanach Bheag
The little yellow place
(936m)

Hill #: **240**

Region #: **05**

Summer Ascent: ☐☐☐☐☐
Winter Ascent: ☐☐☐☐☐

Trailhead: _____

Date:

Time:

Weather:

Companions:

Future Advice:

Beinn na Lap
Mottled hill
(935m)

Summer Ascent: ☐☐☐☐☐
Winter Ascent: ☐☐☐☐☐

Trailhead: _____

Hill #: **241**

Region #: **04**

Date:

Time:

Weather:

Companions:

Future Advice:

_____

_____

_____

_____

_____

_____

_____

_____

_____

_____

_____

_____

_____

Am Basteir
Probably not the executioner?
(934m)

Hill #: 242

Region #: 17

Summer Ascent: ☐☐☐☐☐
Winter Ascent: ☐☐☐☐☐

Trailhead: _____

Date:

Time:

Weather:

Companions:

Future Advice:

_____

_____

_____

_____

_____

_____

_____

_____

_____

_____

_____

_____

Meall a' Chrasgaidh
Hill of the crossing
(934m)

Summer Ascent: ☐☐☐☐☐
Winter Ascent: ☐☐☐☐☐

Trailhead: _____

Hill #: 243

Region #: 14

Date:

Time:

Weather:

Companions:

Future Advice:

Beinn Chabhair
Possibly hill of the hawk
(933m)

Summer Ascent: ☐☐☐☐☐
Winter Ascent: ☐☐☐☐☐

Trailhead: _____

Date:

Time:

Weather:

Companions:

Future Advice:

_____
_____
_____
_____
_____
_____
_____
_____
_____
_____
_____
_____

Fionn Bheinn
Pale-coloured hill
(933m)

Summer Ascent: ☐☐☐☐☐
Winter Ascent: ☐☐☐☐☐

Trailhead: _____

Hill #: **245**

Region #: **14**

Date:

Time:

Weather:

Companions:

Future Advice:

_____

_____

_____

_____

_____

_____

_____

_____

_____

_____

_____

_____

_____

Maol Chean-dearg
Bald red head
(933m)

Summer Ascent: ☐☐☐☐☐
Winter Ascent: ☐☐☐☐☐
Trailhead: _____

Date:

Time:

Weather:

Companions:

Future Advice:

_____

_____

_____

_____

_____

_____

_____

_____

_____

_____

_____

_____

The Cairnwell
Hill of bags (or hill of the peat hags)
(933m)

Summer Ascent: ☐☐☐☐☐

Winter Ascent: ☐☐☐☐☐

Trailhead: _____

Hill #: 247

Region #: 06

Date:

Time:

Weather:

Companions:

Future Advice:

_____
_____
_____
_____
_____
_____
_____
_____
_____
_____
_____
_____
_____

Meall Buidhe
Yellow hill
(932m)

Hill #: 248

Region #: 02

Summer Ascent: ☐☐☐☐☐
Winter Ascent: ☐☐☐☐☐
Trailhead: _____

Date:

Time:

Weather:

Companions:

Future Advice:

_____
_____
_____
_____
_____
_____
_____
_____
_____
_____
_____
_____

Beinn Bhreac
Speckled hill
(931m)

Summer Ascent: ☐☐☐☐☐

Winter Ascent: ☐☐☐☐☐

Hill #: 249

Trailhead: _____

Region #: 08

Date:

Time:

Weather:

Companions:

Future Advice:

_____

_____

_____

_____

_____

_____

_____

_____

_____

_____

_____

_____

Ben Chonzie (Ben-y-Hone)
Mossy hill
(931m)

Hill #: 250

Region #: 01

Summer Ascent: ☐☐☐☐☐
Winter Ascent: ☐☐☐☐☐
Trailhead: _____

Date:

Time:

Weather:

Companions:

Future Advice:

_____
_____
_____
_____
_____
_____
_____
_____
_____
_____
_____
_____
_____

A' Chailleach
The old woman
(930m)

Summer Ascent: ☐☐☐☐☐
Winter Ascent: ☐☐☐☐☐

Trailhead: _____

Hill #: 251

Region #: 09

Date:

Time:

Weather:

Companions:

Future Advice:

Bla Bheinn (Blaven)
Blue hill (or warm hill)
(928m)

Hill #: 252

Region #: 17

Summer Ascent: ☐☐☐☐☐
Winter Ascent: ☐☐☐☐☐
Trailhead: _____

Date:

Time:

Weather:

Companions:

Future Advice:

_____
_____
_____
_____
_____
_____
_____
_____
_____
_____
_____
_____

Mayar
The plain? (or the moon-glow?)
(928m)

Summer Ascent: ☐☐☐☐☐

Winter Ascent: ☐☐☐☐☐

Trailhead: _____

Hill #: 253

Region #: 07

Date:

Time:

Weather:

Companions:

Future Advice:

_____

_____

_____

_____

_____

_____

_____

_____

_____

_____

_____

_____

_____

_____

Meall nan Eun
Hill of the birds
(928m)

Hill #: **254**

Region #: **03**

Summer Ascent: ☐☐☐☐☐
Winter Ascent: ☐☐☐☐☐

Trailhead: _____

Date:

Time:

Weather:

Companions:

Future Advice:

_____

_____

_____

_____

_____

_____

_____

_____

_____

_____

_____

_____

Moruisg
Big water
(928m)

Summer Ascent: ☐☐☐☐☐
Winter Ascent: ☐☐☐☐☐

Trailhead: _____

Hill #: **255**

Region #: **12**

Date:

Time:

Weather:

Companions:

Future Advice:

_____

_____

_____

_____

_____

_____

_____

_____

_____

_____

_____

_____

Ben Hope
Hill of the bay/inlet
(927m)

Summer Ascent: ☐☐☐☐☐
Winter Ascent: ☐☐☐☐☐

Trailhead: _____

Date:

Time:

Weather:

Companions:

Future Advice:

_____
_____
_____
_____
_____
_____
_____
_____
_____
_____
_____
_____

Eididh nan Clach Geala

Web of the white stones (or nest of the...)

(927m)

Summer Ascent: ☐☐☐☐☐

Winter Ascent: ☐☐☐☐☐

Trailhead: _____

Hill #: 257

Region #: 15

Date:

Time:

Weather:

Companions:

Future Advice:

_____

_____

_____

_____

_____

_____

_____

_____

_____

_____

_____

_____

Beinn Liath Mhor
Big grey hill
(926m)

Hill #: 258

Region #: 13

Summer Ascent: ☐☐☐☐☐
Winter Ascent: ☐☐☐☐☐
Trailhead: _____

Date:

Time:

Weather:

Companions:

Future Advice:

_____
_____
_____
_____
_____
_____
_____
_____
_____
_____
_____
_____

Beinn Narnain
Notched hill? (or hill of the notches?)
(926m)

Summer Ascent: ☐☐☐☐☐

Winter Ascent: ☐☐☐☐☐

Hill #: 259

Trailhead: _____

Region #: 01

Date:

Time:

Weather:

Companions:

Future Advice:

Geal Charn
White hill
(926m)

Hill #: 260

Region #: 09

Summer Ascent: ☐☐☐☐☐
Winter Ascent: ☐☐☐☐☐

Trailhead: _____

Date:

Time:

Weather:

Companions:

Future Advice:

_____

_____

_____

_____

_____

_____

_____

_____

_____

_____

_____

_____

Meall a Choire Leith
Hill of the grey corrie
(926m)

Summer Ascent: ☐☐☐☐☐
Winter Ascent: ☐☐☐☐☐

Hill #: 261

Region #: 02

Trailhead: _____

Date:

Time:

Weather:

Companions:

Future Advice:

_____
_____
_____
_____
_____
_____
_____
_____
_____
_____
_____
_____
_____

Seana Bhraigh
Old upper part (or old height)
(926m)

Hill #: 262

Region #: 15

Summer Ascent: ☐☐☐☐☐
Winter Ascent: ☐☐☐☐☐
Trailhead: _____

Date:

Time:

Weather:

Companions:

Future Advice:

_____
_____
_____
_____
_____
_____
_____
_____
_____
_____
_____

Buachaille Etive Beag (Stob Coire Raineach)
Bracken ferny corrie peak
(925m)

Summer Ascent: ☐☐☐☐☐

Winter Ascent: ☐☐☐☐☐

Trailhead: _____

Hill #: 263

Region #: 03

Date:

Time:

Weather:

Companions:

Future Advice:

Creag Pitridh
Petrie's creag? (or cliff/steep face)
(924m)

Hill #: **264**

Region #: **04**

Summer Ascent: ☐☐☐☐☐
Winter Ascent: ☐☐☐☐☐

Trailhead: _____

Date:

Time:

Weather:

Companions:

Future Advice:

_____
_____
_____
_____
_____
_____
_____
_____
_____
_____
_____
_____
_____

Sgurr nan Eag
Peak of the notches
(924m)

Summer Ascent: ☐☐☐☐☐
Winter Ascent: ☐☐☐☐☐

Trailhead: _____

Date:

Time:

Weather:

Companions:

Future Advice:

_____

_____

_____

_____

_____

_____

_____

_____

_____

_____

_____

_____

_____

An Coileachan
The little cock
(923m)

Hill #: 266

Region #: 14

Summer Ascent: ☐☐☐☐☐
Winter Ascent: ☐☐☐☐☐
Trailhead: _____

Date:

Time:

Weather:

Companions:

Future Advice:

_____
_____
_____
_____
_____
_____
_____
_____
_____
_____
_____
_____

Sgurr nan Each
Peak of the horses
(923m)

Summer Ascent: ☐☐☐☐☐
Winter Ascent: ☐☐☐☐☐

Hill #: 267

Region #: 14

Trailhead: _____

Date:

Time:

Weather:

Companions:

Future Advice:

Tom na Gruagaich (Beinn Alligin)
Hill of the maiden
(922m)

Hill #: 268

Region #: 13

Summer Ascent: ☐☐☐☐☐
Winter Ascent: ☐☐☐☐☐
Trailhead: _____

Date:

Time:

Weather:

Companions:

Future Advice:

_____
_____
_____
_____
_____
_____
_____
_____
_____
_____
_____

An Socach
The snout
(921m)

Summer Ascent: ☐☐☐☐☐
Winter Ascent: ☐☐☐☐☐
Trailhead: _____

Date:

Time:

Weather:

Companions:

Future Advice:

Sgiath Chuil
Back wing (or sheltering spot)
(921m)

Summer Ascent: ☐☐☐☐☐
Winter Ascent: ☐☐☐☐☐

Trailhead: _____

Date:

Time:

Weather:

Companions:

Future Advice:

_____

_____

_____

_____

_____

_____

_____

_____

_____

_____

_____

_____

Carn Sgulain
Hill of the basket (or hill of the old man)
(920m)

Summer Ascent: ☐☐☐☐☐
Winter Ascent: ☐☐☐☐☐

Trailhead: _____

Hill #: 271

Region #: 09

Date:

Time:

Weather:

Companions:

Future Advice:

_____
_____
_____
_____
_____
_____
_____
_____
_____
_____
_____
_____

Gairich
Roaring
(919m)

Summer Ascent: ☐☐☐☐☐
Winter Ascent: ☐☐☐☐☐

Trailhead: _____

Date:

Time:

Weather:

Companions:

Future Advice:

_____
_____
_____
_____
_____
_____
_____
_____
_____
_____
_____
_____

Ruadh Stac Mor
Big red peak
(919m)

Summer Ascent: ☐☐☐☐☐
Winter Ascent: ☐☐☐☐☐

Trailhead: _____

Hill #: **273**

Region #: **14**

Date:

Time:

Weather:

Companions:

Future Advice:

A' Ghlas-bheinn
The greenish-grey hill
(918m)

Hill #: **274**

Region #: **11**

Summer Ascent: ☐☐☐☐☐
Winter Ascent: ☐☐☐☐☐
Trailhead: _____

Date:

Time:

Weather:

Companions:

Future Advice:

_____
_____
_____
_____
_____
_____
_____
_____
_____
_____
_____
_____

Creag nan Damh
Rock of the stags
(918m)

Summer Ascent: ☐☐☐☐☐
Winter Ascent: ☐☐☐☐☐

Trailhead: _____

Hill #: 275

Region #: 10

Date:

Time:

Weather:

Companions:

Future Advice:

Meall na Teanga
Hill of the tongue
(918m)

Summer Ascent: ☐☐☐☐☐
Winter Ascent: ☐☐☐☐☐
Trailhead: _____

Date:

Time:

Weather:

Companions:

Future Advice:

_____
_____
_____
_____
_____
_____
_____
_____
_____
_____
_____
_____

Sgurr a' Mhadaidh
Peak of the fox
(918m)

Summer Ascent: ☐☐☐☐☐

Winter Ascent: ☐☐☐☐☐

Trailhead: _____

Date:

Time:

Weather:

Companions:

Future Advice:

_____

_____

_____

_____

_____

_____

_____

_____

_____

_____

_____

_____

Geal-charn
White hill
(917m)

Summer Ascent: ☐☐☐☐☐
Winter Ascent: ☐☐☐☐☐

Trailhead: _____

Date:

Time:

Weather:

Companions:

Future Advice:

_____

_____

_____

_____

_____

_____

_____

_____

_____

_____

_____

_____

Beinn a' Chleibh
Hill of the creel (or Hill of the chest)
(916m)

Summer Ascent: ☐☐☐☐☐

Winter Ascent: ☐☐☐☐☐

Trailhead: _____

Date:

Time:

Weather:

Companions:

Future Advice:

_____

_____

_____

_____

_____

_____

_____

_____

_____

_____

_____

_____

Ben Vane
Middle hill
(916m)

Hill #: 280

Region #: 01

Summer Ascent: ☐☐☐☐☐
Winter Ascent: ☐☐☐☐☐
Trailhead: _____

Date:

Time:

Weather:

Companions:

Future Advice:

_____
_____
_____
_____
_____
_____
_____
_____
_____
_____
_____
_____

Beinn Teallach
Forge hill (or hearth hill)
(915m)

Summer Ascent: ☐☐☐☐☐

Winter Ascent: ☐☐☐☐☐

Trailhead: _____

Hill #: **281**

Region #: **09**

Date:

Time:

Weather:

Companions:

Future Advice:

_____

_____

_____

_____

_____

_____

_____

_____

_____

_____

_____

_____

Carn Aosda
Hill of age (or ancient hill)
(915m)

Hill #: 282

Region #: 06

Summer Ascent: ☐☐☐☐☐
Winter Ascent: ☐☐☐☐☐
Trailhead: _____

Date:

Time:

Weather:

Companions:

Future Advice:

_____
_____
_____
_____
_____
_____
_____
_____
_____
_____
_____
_____

Disclaimer:

DISCLAIMER:

Climbing any munro is difficult and dangerous. If you decide to partake in this dangerous activity you do so at your own risk and assume any/all consequences involved. Under no circumstance are the Wee Munro Team, its members and/or partners, accountable for any consequences that may arise (including but not limited to: harm, damage, theft, legal liability, death, parking fines, trespassing fines, camping fines, etc…).

Scottish Outdoor Access Code:

This book is made available by the Wee Munro Team for informational purposes only. It provides general information about access rights according to open source Government information. Whenever you exercise your access rights you should do so with a full understanding of the laws and repercussions associated with such actions.

Please note:

The purpose of this book is to supply the hiking/hill walking community with a useful item for a hiking trip. We aim for this book to encourage you to act responsibly and be mindful in your approach to the outdoors, whilst providing you with a sentimental keepsake.

We aim to make products that are accessible to all. As such, we try to keep the price as low as possible: we print in black and white, keep inventory low and never accept paid placements. The freedom of this book depends on people purchasing it and donating to the cause. Our profit on each book is measured in pence, not pounds. If you would like to donate please reach out to us at:

weemunroteam@gmail.com

See you on the next trail friend,

Wee Munro Team

*If you or someone you know is planning to hike the West Highland Way, point them in the direction of our West Highland Way book. Available on Amazon and in select stores.

Alphabetical Index

Alphabetical Index

Alphabetical Index

Alphabetical Index

Alphabetical Index

Regional Index

Regional Index

Regional Index

Regional Index

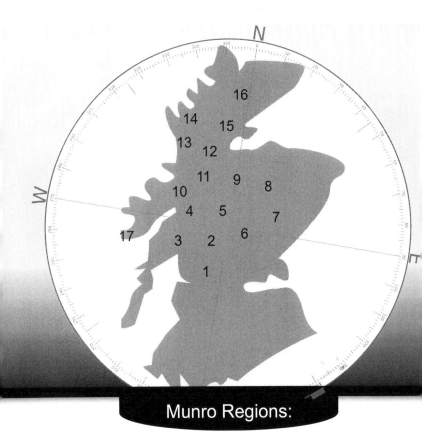

Munro Regions:

1. Loch Fyre to Loch Tay
2. Loch Tay to Rannoch Moor
3. Rannoch Moor to Loch Linnhe
4. Loch Linnhe to Loch Ericht
5. Loch Ericht to Drumochter
6. Drumochter to Glen Shee
7. Glen Carron to Loch Linnhe
8. The Cairngorms (Deeside to Speyside)
9. Speyside to Great Glen
10. Loch Linnhe to Glen Shiel
11. Glen Shiel to Loch Mullardoch
12. Loch Mullardoch to Glen Carron
13. Glen Carron to Loch Maree
14. Loch Maree to Loch Broom
15. Loch Broom to the Cromarty Firth
16. Loch Broom to the Pentland Firth
17. The Isles

Hello again friend,

You've come to the end of our book. This could mean you are sitting in a rainy tent surrounded by breathtaking peaks and are looking for a little reading. Perhaps you are on a bus and forgot your book- the only thing close was our wonderful book and here you are. Maybe, even better, you love the book so much you wanted to read each page from start to finish…

Either way, we just wanted to say, the only way this book remains alive and up-to-date is people sending us their knowledge. Please let us know where we've gone wrong, mistakes we've made and things you think we've forgotten. We'd love to edit it for the next edition. Email us at:

weemunroteam@gmail.com.

We'll see you on the next trail,

Wee Munro Team